GW01463926

EARTH AND SPACE

Written by

Martin Lunn

Illustrated by

Brigid Collins, Line & Line,
The Maltings Partnership and Steve Noon

CONTENTS

The Sun

It is not surprising that many ancient civilisations regarded the Sun as a god. It is the largest and brightest object in the sky and its appearance in the morning chases away the darkness of night. The ancient Egyptians called their sun god Ra. The ancient Greeks and Romans believed in the same sun god – he was called Apollo.

The Sun is a huge ball of burning gases. It appears so large in the sky because it is very much bigger than the Earth and it is close by. The Sun totally rules the Solar System. If the Sun was not there, we would not be here. There would be no Earth. The Sun provides light and heat without which life cannot exist.

Did you know?

The Sun is about 150 million km from the Earth.

Its diameter is about 1.4 million km.

The temperature in its centre is about 14 million °C.

The Egyptian sun god, Ra

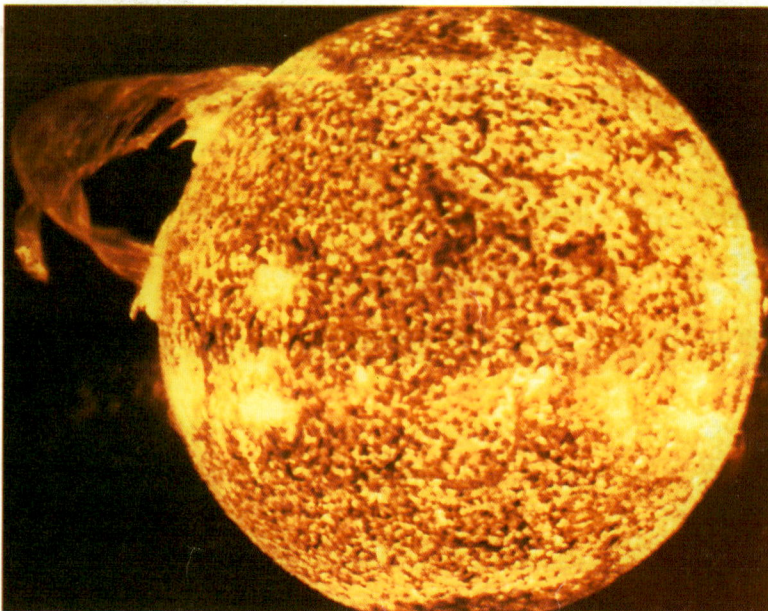

This 'flame' is called a solar flare

Suns and stars

The Sun is a star and is very similar to many of the other stars we can see in the night sky. All stars are suns, so we could say that our Sun is our local star. If we were to journey out to the stars and look back towards the Sun, it would look no different from the other tiny dots we see in the sky.

Some stars are younger than our Sun, some older. At present our Sun is about 'middle-aged'. It will eventually use up all its gases and will 'die'. Luckily for us it still has about another 5000 million years' worth of gases left!

The Sun has a surface temperature of about 6000°C. The hottest stars have surface temperatures of over 50 000°C, the coolest are about 2600°C.

People sometimes say 'red sky at night, sailors' delight' because they think a dramatic red sunset means tomorrow will be a nice day

Safety first

You must be very wary of the Sun. It is very hot and bright. You must never look directly at the Sun through a telescope or binoculars. You will blind yourself if you do. Even staring at the Sun can cause blindness.

Sun observations

The Sun rises in the east and sets in the west, so during the day the Sun appears to move across the sky. This movement is not along a straight flat line; the Sun appears over the horizon and then climbs up the sky during the morning and drops down towards the horizon again in the afternoon.

Shadows through the day

Shadows can tell us about the Sun's position. Shadows are long when the Sun is low in the sky; they are short when the Sun is high in the sky. Shadows are shorter at midday than in the morning or evening.

A shadow stick is a piece of wood either permanently placed in the ground or attached to a base as part of a moveable system. The Sun must be shining brightly enough to cast a sharp shadow. If the shadow stick is kept in one place, the length and position its shadow can be measured at different times of the day.

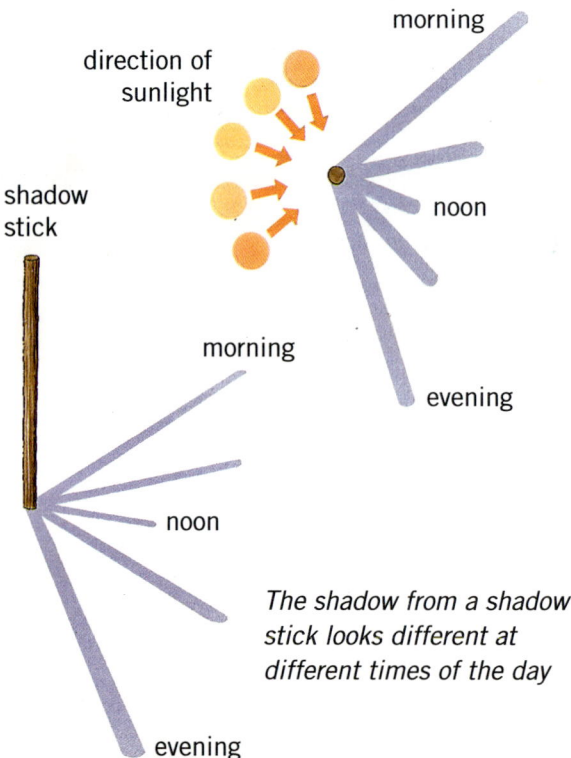

Sundials are really shadow sticks for telling the time

The shadow moves round the stick during the day. The position and length of the shadow changes because the Earth is spinning and the position of the Sun appears to have moved.

Understanding shadows enabled people to make sundials. The shadow cast by the shadow stick or gnomon falls onto a scale so you can tell the time.

Shadows through the year

The height of the Sun in the sky changes through the year as well as through the day. This is because the Earth moves round the Sun. In the United Kingdom, shadows are shortest in June and longest in December because the Sun is highest in the sky in June and at its lowest in December. In Australia, the shortest shadows occur in December and the longest in June.

The shadow from a shadow stick looks different at different times of the day

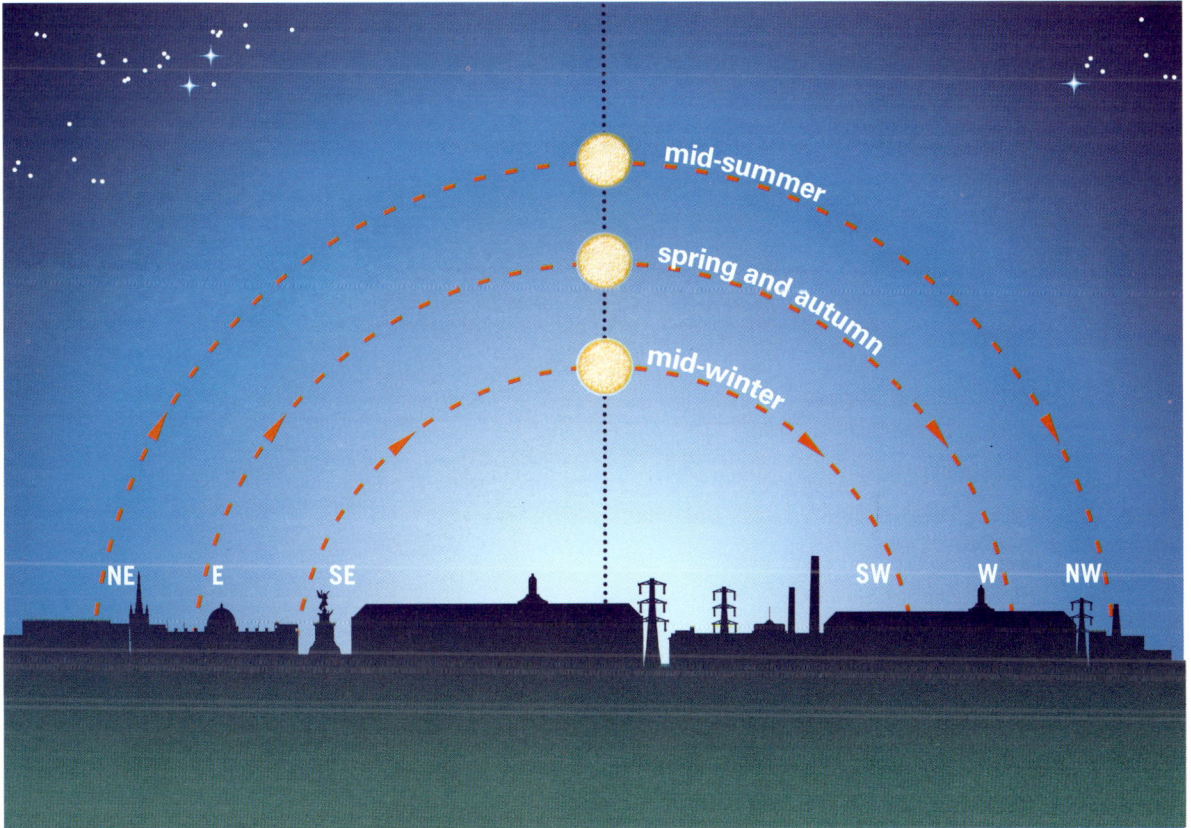

The path of the Sun in the sky changes with the time of year (you are facing south)

Measuring the Earth

Greek scientists of 2500 years ago observed the Sun and made calculations about the size of the Earth. Their estimates in 240 BC were better than those used by Christopher Columbus in 1492. Columbus was looking for India when he found America. The Earth was bigger than he thought!

This gnomon (shadow stick) was used by astronauts on the Moon to measure the position of the Sun

Day and night

Our planet is called the Earth, it is a sphere or ball of rock that travels around the Sun in its own particular path. This path is called the Earth's orbit. At the same time, the Earth is spinning. It spins all the time, around an imaginary line passing through its centre from the North Pole to the South Pole. This imaginary line is called the Earth's axis.

The Sun is shining all the time, even when we can't see it. It is the spinning of the Earth that causes day and night. It is daytime when your side of the Earth is facing towards the Sun. It is night when your side of the Earth is facing away from the Sun.

The side of the Earth facing the Sun has daytime

Turning night into day

Throughout history daytime has been seen as a period of safety and night as a time of danger.

In the very earliest times, people used to strike two sharp stones together to make sparks, then they could light fires. By Roman times, people could light their homes using lamps with vegetable oil or animal fat. During the Middle Ages, people knew how to make and use candles to provide light. A hundred years ago, people used gas lamps. Today we use electric light bulbs.

Daytime and the 24-hour day

The Earth takes 24 hours to spin round once. Astronomers call this period of time a day. This can be confusing because in that 24-hour day we have the time we usually call a day (when it is light) and the time we usually call night (when it is dark). An ordinary day plus a night equals an 'astronomical day'.

Although we now know that day and night are caused by the Earth spinning, there have been many different beliefs as to why there is day and night.

The ancient Greeks and Romans believed the sun god Apollo drove his chariot across the sky in the day and rested at night

Day and night on other planets

All the planets in the Solar System have day and night because they all spin. Some of them take longer than the Earth to spin round once and some take less time. The ones that take longer have daylight and night for a longer time than the Earth. The ones that take less time have daylight and night for less time.

Day and night on Saturn

The seasons

The ancient Egyptians thought that the Earth took one year (12 months or 365 days) to orbit once round the Sun. We now know that an Earth year is a bit longer – 365.25 days. Each year has four seasons, spring, summer, autumn and winter.

The Earth is divided into two halves, the northern and southern hemispheres, by an imaginary line round the middle called the equator. The Earth does not 'sit' upright in space, it is tilted over to one side by 23.4°. As the Earth moves round the Sun, this tilt never changes. First one hemisphere is tilted towards the Sun then, when the Earth is on the other side of the Sun, the other hemisphere is tilted towards it.

Summer and winter

When the hemisphere you live in is tilted towards the Sun, you can see the Sun for longer, there is more light and heat and it is summer. Six months later, your hemisphere will be tilting away from the Sun so you will receive less light and heat. This is when you have winter. In between are spring and autumn.

The Earth spins once in 24 hours whether it is winter or summer. In summer when your hemisphere is tilted towards the Sun, it appears to be higher in the sky and the days are very long. In the winter, the Sun appears to be much lower in the sky and the days are shorter.

All the planets go round the Sun and they all have four seasons.

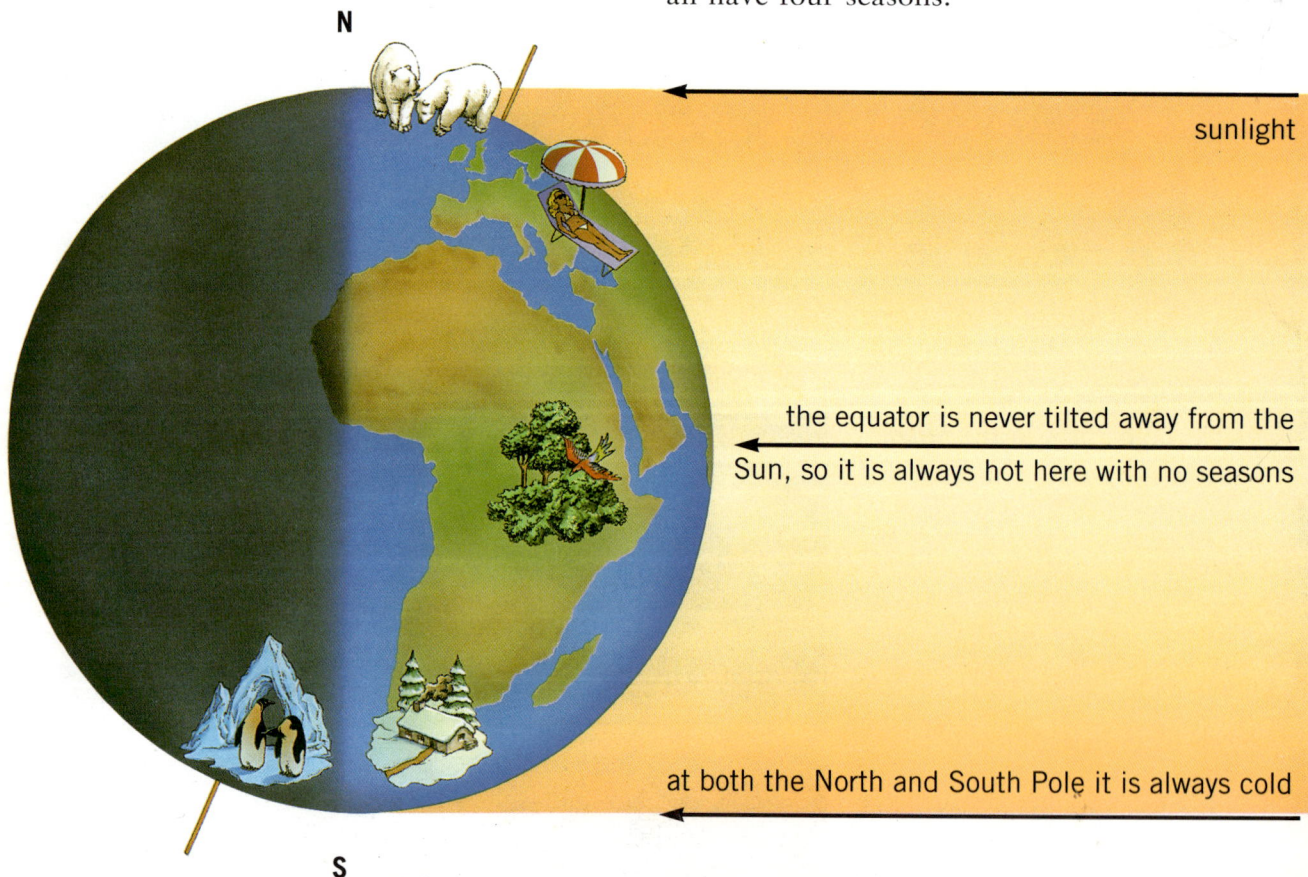

N

sunlight

the equator is never tilted away from the Sun, so it is always hot here with no seasons

at both the North and South Pole it is always cold

S

When it is summer in the northern hemisphere, it is winter in the southern hemisphere

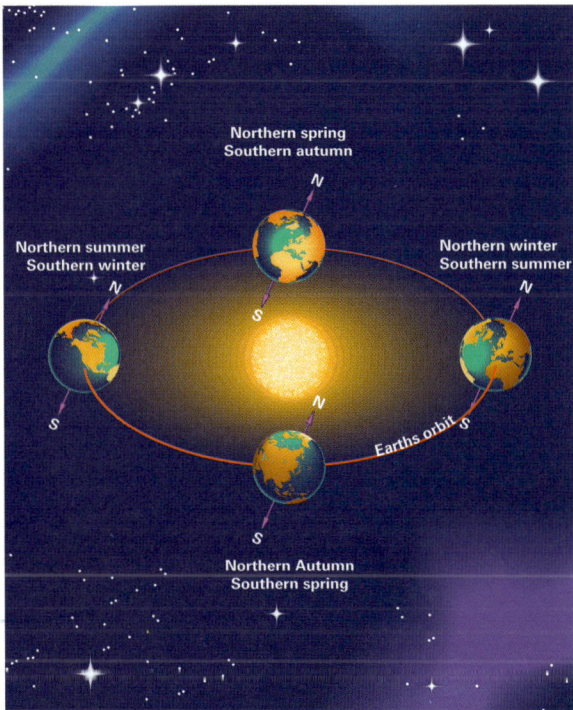

What season it is depends on whether or not your hemisphere is tilted towards the Sun

North and south

The length of daytime is also affected by how far north or south of the equator you live. In June, the United Kingdom has about 15 hours of daylight. Further north, you can still see the Sun in the time we usually call night. This is called the midnight sun. At the North Pole during summer it is always light because the Sun never sets. At the same time of year, New Zealand has only about 8 hours of daylight and at the South Pole the Sun can't be seen at all because the South Pole is tilted too far away from the Sun.

Six months later, the southern hemisphere has the longer periods of daylight during its summer, while we have winter. In our winter the Sun can't be seen at the North Pole, but is always visible at the South Pole where it is summer.

Cycle of seasons				
Northern hemisphere	spring	summer	autumn	winter
Southern hemisphere	autumn	winter	spring	summer

In the northern hemisphere, you have to travel a long way north in summer to see the midnight sun

The Moon

The full moon

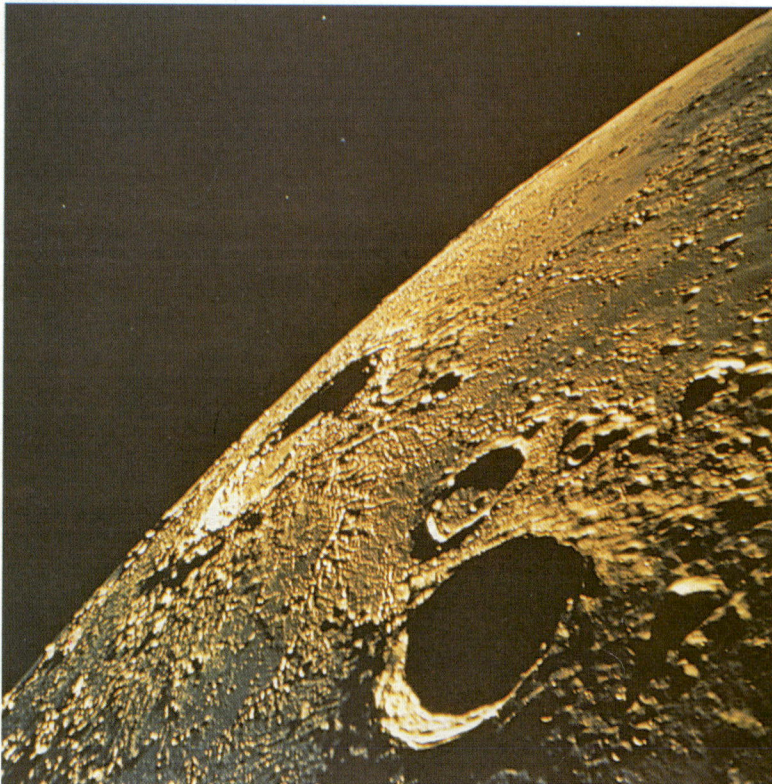

The Moon is our closest neighbour in space. It is a ball of rock that orbits the Earth. It is Earth's only natural satellite.

After the Sun, the Moon appears as the biggest and brightest object in the night sky. However, appearances can be deceptive. The Moon seems to be so large because it is very close to us in space terms. In fact, it is only about one-quarter the size of the Earth.

The Moon has no light of its own. We see it because it reflects sunlight. Moonlight is reflected sunlight.

The Moon's surface is covered by dents or holes called craters. These are mainly caused by lumps of rock crashing onto the Moon's surface.

The Moon is the only other place in the Universe visited by human beings. In 1969 Neil Armstrong and Buzz Aldrin became the first people to walk on the Moon. So far 12 men have visited the Moon but no women.

The crater furthest away is one of the biggest on the Moon and is called Copernicus

Atmosphere

The Earth is surrounded by layers of air. These layers are called Earth's atmosphere. The Moon does not have an atmosphere. It is airless and there is no wind or rain. If you go for a walk on a beach, you leave footprints in the sand. Later, the tide comes in and washes them away. Or, if the sand is dry, the wind might blow sand into your footprints and cover them up. But if you visited the Moon, you would still be able to see the astronauts' footprints from 1969. The footprints made by the astronauts and the craters made by rocks will remain on the Moon's surface for ever because there is no atmosphere on the Moon.

There is nothing to remove these footprints from the Moon's surface

Moon myths

Ancient civilisations considered the Moon as a god and today there are still many interesting and unusual stories, jokes and legends about the Moon. For instance, that it is made of 'green cheese', that you might go mad when there is a full moon, and that certain unfortunate people turn into werewolves on the night of the full moon!

Werewolves only appear when there is a full moon!

Moonwatch

If you have a pair of binoculars, you can use them to look at the Moon. When you look at the Moon, you can see some grey areas. These are mountains and craters which make the 'Man in the Moon's face'. (Do not try this at the full moon as it can be painfully bright.)

Have you noticed that sometimes you can see the Moon during the day as well as at night?

The Moon is about to be 'eclipsed' by this hot air balloon!

Why does the Moon appear to change shape?

The Moon takes 29.5 days to orbit round the Earth. It takes the same time to rotate once on its own axis. In this time its appearance changes. This is because light from the Sun always illuminates half of the Moon, but sometimes the illuminated half of the Moon is facing away from us.

When the Moon is between the Sun and Earth, its dark side is turned towards us. When this happens we cannot see the Moon and we say there is a new moon. But when the Earth is between the Sun and the Moon, we see the lighted side of the Moon. When we can see *all* of the lighted side, we say there is a full moon. In between times, we see part of the lighted side; sometimes we can see a lot of it, sometimes only a little. The different shapes or phases of the Moon have names such as a crescent moon and a gibbous moon.

We never see the far side of the Moon. This is because it takes the Moon the same time to rotate on its axis as it takes it to orbit the Earth.

Sun's rays

7

8   6

1   Earth   5

2   4

3

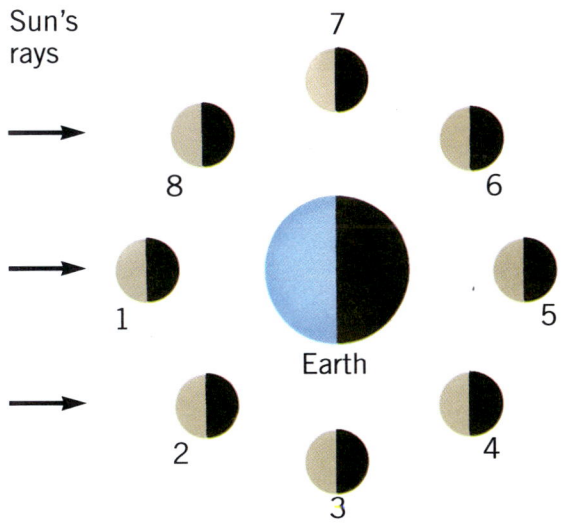

Phase of the Moon	Time of day when seen
1 new moon	(not seen)
2 waxing crescent	most of the day and early evening
3 first quarter	afternoon and first half of the night
4 waxing gibbous	evening and most of the night
5 full moon	all night
6 waning gibbous	most of the night and early morning
7 last quarter	second half of the night and morning
8 waning crescent	before sunrise and most of the day
9 new moon	(not seen)

Why we don't see the far side of the Moon

Try sitting on a stool (you are the Earth) and ask a friend to walk round you as the Moon. Your friend must keep looking at you all the time so you always see your friend's face but never see the back of your friend's head. In the time that your friend has walked round you, he or she has also turned round themselves once. Try this slowly and you will see how your friend turns round to always face you. This is how the Moon behaves.

Eclipses

Eclipses happen because the Earth and the Moon cast shadows. Try taking a ball outside on a sunny day and throwing it against a wall. As the ball moves, so does its shadow. The shadow the ball casts on the ground or wall is like the shadow the Moon casts on the Earth.

When the Moon passes between the Earth and the Sun so that the Sun, Moon and Earth form a straight line in that order, the Moon casts a shadow on the Earth. This is called an eclipse of the Sun or a solar eclipse. If you are standing in the Moon's shadow, you can see the Sun gradually disappear then reappear as the Moon passes in front of it.

In a solar eclipse the Moon hides the Sun

When the Earth passes between the Sun and the Moon so that the Sun, Earth and Moon are in a straight line in that order, the Earth casts a shadow on the Moon. This is called an eclipse of the Moon or a lunar eclipse. The Moon is not hidden during a lunar eclipse, it turns a coppery red as the Earth's shadow falls on it.

Predicting eclipses

We do not have eclipses of the Sun and Moon every month. The Moon orbits the Earth at an angle so they do not often form a straight line with the Sun. However, because we know about the movements of the Earth and the Moon, we can predict when eclipses are going to occur.

In a lunar eclipse the Moon turns a coppery red

Viewing a solar eclipse

Even during an eclipse of the Sun you must not look directly at the Sun through binoculars or a telescope. To be safe, you can stand under a leafy tree and look at the ground. As the Moon passes in front of the Sun, you will see lots of images of the dark circle of the Moon with light from the Sun behind it.

A dangerous dragon

In ancient China it was believed that a solar eclipse was caused by an unfriendly dragon (the Moon) passing in front of the Sun and trying to eat it.
To prevent this and to scare the dragon away, as much noise as possible was made by banging drums, beating gongs and shouting. It always worked!

A safe way to view a solar eclipse

Discovering the planets

In ancient times astronomers noticed that there were five stars that wandered about the sky. These are planets. The word 'planet' comes from the Greek verb 'to wander'.

The planets Uranus, Neptune and Pluto were not discovered until the telescope was invented. The ancient astronomers did not know about them because they are too far away to be seen without optical aids.

Like the Moon, the planets do not produce light. They reflect some of the sunlight that reaches them. This is why they shine.

The first five planets

Like the ancient astronomers, you can see the bright planets without the help of binoculars or a telescope. They are not all visible at the same time because they have different orbits. Newspapers produce charts and information about the night sky at the end of each month. This will tell you which planets you can see.

▶ Mercury is difficult to see because it appears close to the Sun. It looks like a bright pinkish star. Look for it when the Sun has just set.

◀ Venus is the brightest of the planets. It is sometimes called the morning star or the evening star because it is in the eastern sky before sunrise or the western sky after sunset. But remember, it is a planet not a star.

◄

Mars is very red. Occasionally (when it comes very close to Earth) it becomes the second brightest planet.

Jupiter is usually the second brightest planet. If you have a pair of binoculars, you can sometimes see up to four of Jupiter's largest moons.

▼

How long is a year?

Some planets have years that are longer than ours, and some are shorter. Each planet travels round the Sun in its own orbit. The length of time a planet takes to go round the Sun once is called its year. The planets that are closer to the Sun have much shorter orbits than the planets that are further away. This means they have shorter years.

◄

Saturn is the most distant planet you can see without a telescope. It is not so bright as the others. It looks like a dirty yellow star.

Facts and figures about the planets

Name	Distance from Sun (km)	Diameter (km)	Time taken to spin once (Earth time)	Time taken to go round Sun once (Earth time)	Surface temperature (°C)	Number of moons or satellites
Mercury	58 million	4878	58d 15h 36m	88d	−180 to +430	0
Venus	108 million	12 102	243d 0h 14m	225d	465	0
Earth	150 million	12 756	23h 56m 04s	365.25d	15	1
Mars	228 million	6786	24h 37m 48s	687.98d	−133 to +22	2
Jupiter	778 million	142 984	9h 55m 30s	11.8yr	−150	16
Saturn	1427 million	120 536	10h 39m 22s	29.4yr	−180	18
Uranus	2871 million	51 118	17h 14m	84yr	−210	15
Neptune	4497 million	49 528	16h 7m	164.7yr	−210	8
Pluto	5914 million	2284	6d 9h 18m	248.5yr	−220	1

(yr = years, d = days, h = hours, m = minutes, s = seconds)

Planets and gods

The five 'wandering stars' were named after gods: Mercury was the messenger, Venus was the goddess of love, Mars was the god of war, Jupiter was the ruler of the gods, and Saturn was the father of Jupiter.

When the remaining three planets were discovered they were also named after gods to fit in with the others. Neptune was the god of the sea. Uranus was the oldest of all the gods and was the father of Saturn. Pluto was the god of the underworld. The Earth is the odd one out, it is the only planet not named after a god. This is because it is the one we live on.

Uranus was discovered by William Herschel in 1781, 170 years after the astronomical telescope was invented.

After another 65 years, in 1846, Johann Galle and Heinrich D'Arrest discovered Neptune.

Cylde Tombaugh discovered Pluto in 1930. He made the discovery as a result of mathematical calculations. This photograph was taken by the Hubble Space Telescope; it is the only picture we have of Pluto.

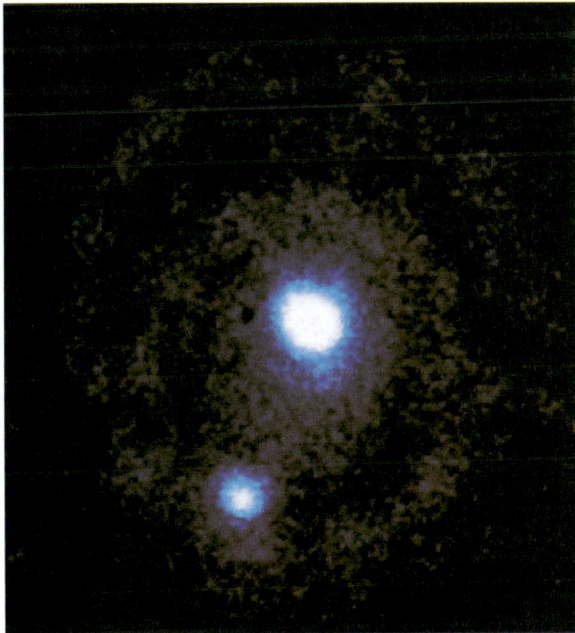

The Solar System

The Earth is one of nine planets orbiting the star called the Sun. Some of the planets have satellites or moons orbiting them. The Sun, the planets and their moons, the asteroids, comets and other small pieces of dust, make up what we call the Solar System.

The inner planets

The four inner planets are Mercury, Venus, Earth and Mars. They are all small and rocky bodies. They have very few moons or none at all.

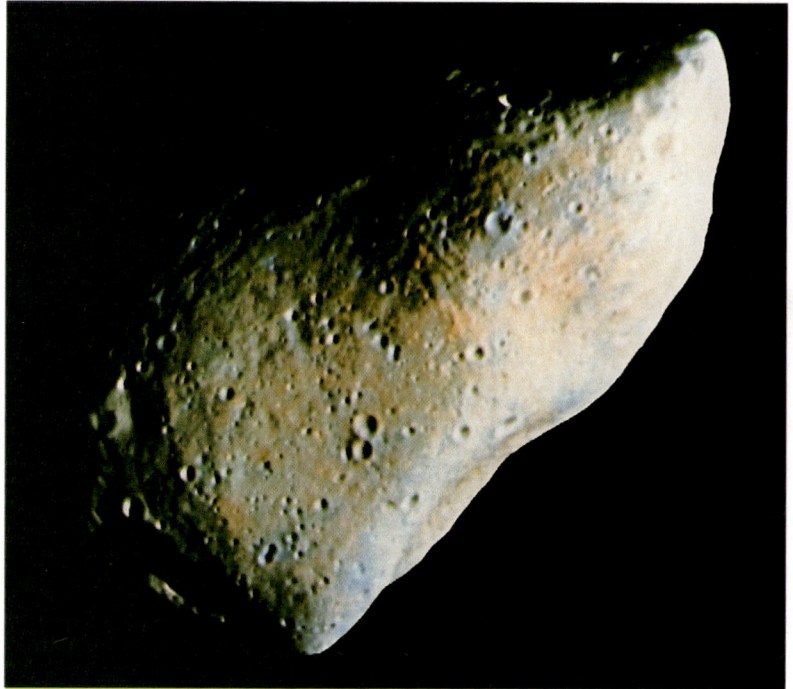

This asteroid is called Gaspra

Asteroids

Beyond Mars is the asteroid belt. It is made up of thousands of lumps of rock that orbit the Sun together. Asteroids are as old as the rest of the Solar System.

The outer planets

There are four large outer planets. They are often called gas giants. Jupiter, Saturn, Uranus and Neptune are all large spheres of gas. They are much colder than the inner planets. They all have large families of satellites or moons.

In 1930, Pluto was found. It is the outermost planet and is not a gas giant. It is a small world which appears to be made of ice and rock. It is the only planet which no space probe has visited.

Comets

Comets are minor members of the Solar System. They are lumps of rock, dust trapped in ice. They look a bit like snowballs that are full of dirt and grit and are often called 'dirty snowballs'.

Halley's Comet is the most famous and brightest comet

Meteors and meteorites

Meteors are tiny pieces of dust which orbit the Sun. Sometimes they rush into the Earth's atmosphere and burn up. When this happens you can see streaks of light in the night sky. Rather confusingly these are often called shooting stars. At certain times of the year the Earth passes through dense clouds of dust and we experience meteor showers.

Meteorites are rocks large enough not to burn up in the Earth's atmosphere. The last big one was about 20 metres across and entered the atmosphere in 1908. It destroyed over 2000 square kilometres of forest when it exploded 5 miles above northern Siberia.

The five largest asteroids

Name	Diameter (km)
Ceres	1003
Pallas	608
Vesta	538
Hygeia	450
Euphrosyne	370

This meteor was photographed in Canada at dusk

Meteor showers

Shower name	When to look for shooting stars
Quadrantids	January 3–4
Lyrids	April 22
Eta Aquarids	May 4–5
Delta Aquarids	July 28–31
Perseids	August 12–13
Orionids	October 21
Leonids	November 17
Geminids	December 13–14

The stars

Take a look at the night sky on a good clear night. The stars you see are suns just like ours only much further away, that is why they appear so small.

On a clear night from anywhere on Earth it is possible to see about 2500 stars without the help of a pair of binoculars or a telescope.

Stars are formed in clouds of gas that are sometimes called stellar nurseries. The Orion Nebula is one of these. The star map on page 31 will help you find it.

Stars go through different stages and then die. Some finish their lives very quietly; others explode into a very bright star called a supernova before fading.

Star types

There are lots of different star types and sizes. Small stars are called dwarfs and the large ones are called giants. The very large ones are called supergiants. If you look very carefully at the stars, you can see that they are different colours.

The star colours tell astronomers how hot a star is. The stars which appear blue or white in the sky are much hotter than those which appear red. Our Sun is a yellow dwarf.

Galaxies

Galaxies are groups of millions of stars. Some galaxies are called spiral galaxies because of their shape, but when a spiral galaxy is viewed from the side, it looks rather like two fried eggs back to back.

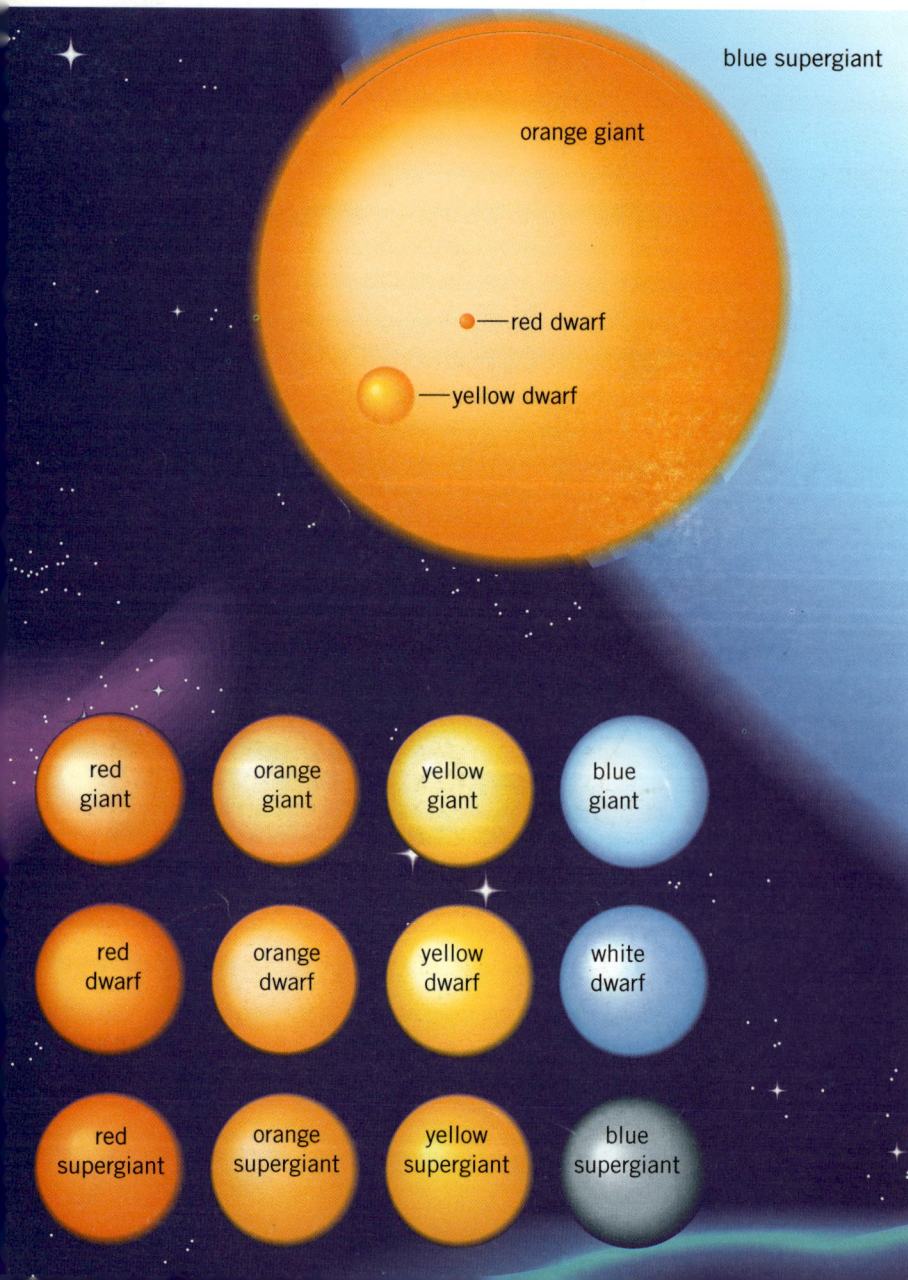

blue supergiant

orange giant

red dwarf

yellow dwarf

red giant	orange giant	yellow giant	blue giant
red dwarf	orange dwarf	yellow dwarf	white dwarf
red supergiant	orange supergiant	yellow supergiant	blue supergiant

These twelve types of star are all different sizes

Seeing stars

In the daytime we can only see one star, the Sun. The other stars are there – we just can't see them because the light from the Sun is so bright that it overwhelms the fainter light from the stars.

Stars don't really twinkle, but they do appear to. This is due to the Earth's atmosphere. The starlight has to pass through the atmosphere before reaching the ground. The layers of air that make up our atmosphere are always moving, so the light from a star seems to move about slightly. This movement is the twinkle.

Navigating

The stars can be used as a compass. If you can find the Great Bear or Plough in the sky, you can then find the Pole Star. This is very useful because the Pole Star tells you where north is. The map on page 29 will help you find the Plough and the Pole Star.

The Orion Nebula is an area where stars are formed

M74(NGC 628) is a spiral galaxy about 30 million light years away

Solar System and star trivia

Earth
Our home is often called the Blue Planet. This is because it has a lot of water in the oceans and looks blue from space.

Mercury
Only one spacecraft, Mariner 10, has visited Mercury. Before that, the best drawings of the planet were made in France during the 1930s. Some of the areas on Mercury were given very strange names, such as 'The Wilderness of Hermes the Thrice Greatest'!

Sun

Venus
This is the only planet named after a female god or goddess. It is not the closest planet to the Sun, but it is the hottest. It has a thick atmosphere that keeps heat in. The Venusian day is longer than the Venusian year. Venus and Uranus are the only planets to spin in a clockwise direction.

Mars
Mars has ice caps that seem to be frozen carbon dioxide. It also has the largest known volcano in the Solar System, Olympus Mons, which is 600 km across and 24 km high.

Jupiter
The largest planet in the Solar System has the shortest day because it spins very fast. A day on Jupiter lasts 9 hours and 55 minutes of Earth time. Ganymede is Jupiter's largest moon, it is also the largest moon in the Solar System and is bigger than Mercury or Pluto. Like Saturn, Jupiter has rings but we can't see them from Earth.

The stars
The largest stars are called supergiants, the smallest are dwarfs. A supergiant is almost as big as the Solar System. A white dwarf is about the same size as Pluto.

Neutron stars are the result of a supernova explosion. They have diameters of about 30 km.

The Sun
The Sun sometimes has black dots on its surface. These are sun spots and are cooler areas on the Sun. Many sun spots are larger than the Earth!

Saturn

Photographs of Saturn taken from Earth show Saturn's rings. The rings look solid but they are made of millions of very tiny particles that orbit round Saturn.

Neptune

This is the windiest planet in the Solar System. It has wind speeds reaching 2000 km/h. Neptune has rings but we can't see them from Earth.

Uranus

This planet is tipped over on its side at an angle of 98° and, like Venus, it spins clockwise. Uranus also has rings but we can't see them from Earth.

The Solar System

The Solar System is mainly empty space.

Pluto

Pluto is the smallest planet in the Solar System and is farthest from the Sun.

Constellations and mythology

In the past, astronomers drew patterns among the stars and gave the patterns the names of heroes and villains. The stars in each pattern or constellation have no special connection. They just happen to be in the same part of the sky.

The ancient Greek astronomers knew 48 constellations. Today we know 88. The new ones are mainly in the southern hemisphere. The Greeks didn't know about them because they didn't travel there.

Orion the Hunter

Orion is a splendid constellation. Orion was a hunter who boasted that he could kill any living creature. Unfortunately, he forgot about the scorpion which stung him on the ankle and killed him.

Orion and the Scorpion are both in the sky, but the gods decided that they should never meet again. In the northern hemisphere, Orion is in the winter sky, and the Scorpion is in the summer sky.

Orion and Scorpio never meet

Perseus rescues Andromeda from the sea monster

Cassiopea

All the characters in Cassiopea's story can be found in the sky. Queen Cassiopea was very boastful and one day she upset Neptune, the king of the sea. He sent a sea monster called Cetus to attack Cassiopea's land. The only way Cassiopea could prevent disaster was to chain her daughter Andromeda to a rock for Cetus to eat. At the last minute, Perseus arrived on the winged horse, Pegasus. Perseus was carrying the Medusa's head and when Cetus looked at it, the monster was turned to stone. In this way Perseus rescued Andromeda whom he then married.

The Great Bear

The Great Bear or Plough can only be seen in the northern hemisphere. Its story is about Callisto and Arcas.

Callisto was very beautiful and had a son called Arcas. Juno, the queen of the gods, was very jealous of Callisto's beauty and turned her into a bear. Many years later, Arcas was out hunting and was about to shoot a bear, because he didn't know it was really Callisto. Jupiter, the king of the gods, saved Callisto by turning Arcas into a bear too. He then caught both animals by the tails, and swung them up into the sky. That is why the Great Bear (Callisto) and the Little Bear (Arcas) have long tails.

Naming the new constellations

The southern constellations were mainly discovered by European explorers in the seventeenth and eighteenth centuries. These constellations were often named after new scientific instruments such as the microscope and the telescope.

The Great Bear and the Little Bear

Signposts in the sky: the Great Bear

The Great Bear or Plough is visible all year. The dashed lines on the star map are the lines you imagine in the sky to help you find other stars.

Finding Polaris

First find the Great Bear. Now you can find Polaris, the Pole Star. Imagine a line drawn from Merak through Dubhe and then carrying on till you reach a bright star on its own. This is Polaris.

Finding Cassiopea

Now imagine a line from Alioth through Polaris. Carry on for some distance on the far side of Polaris. You will reach five bright stars arranged in a rough 'W'. This is the constellation Cassiopeia.

Finding Capella

If you imagine a line from Megrez through Dubhe and keep going, you will eventually come to Capella. On winter evenings Capella is high up and may pass directly overhead. On summer evenings Capella is at its lowest and almost reaches the horizon. Capella is yellowish and is accompanied by a small triangle of stars close by.

Finding Vega

You can find Vega by imagining a line from Phad, to Megrez and then curving out and carrying on till you reach a star that looks blue. This is Vega.

Finding Castor and Pollux

The twins Castor and Pollux can be found by imagining of a line from Megrez through Merak and carrying on until you find the two stars close together. Castor and Pollux can only be seen in winter.

Finding Arcturus and Spica

Arcturus is orange and about as bright as Capella or Vega. To find Arcturus, you must imagine a line from Mizar through Alkaid and then curve downwards. If you continue along the curve past Arcturus you will find another bright star, Spica. Arcturus and Spica can be seen in spring and early summer.

Names and names

The stars were named by many peoples, including the Chinese, Indians and Aztecs. Different civilisations have different names for the same group. We still use the names given by the peoples of the Mediterranean. But sometimes we translate them into English, and sometimes we have other names as well. For example, we often call Ursa Major, the Great Bear. We also call it the Plough. In America, it is called the Big Dipper.

CASSIOPEA

VEGA

POLARIS

CAPELLA

MIZAR

DUBHE

MEGREZ

ALKAID

ALIOTH

MERAK

CASTOR

PHAD

POLLUX

ARCTURUS

REGULUS

SPICA

Signposts in the sky: Orion

Orion can only be seen in winter and all its chief stars are brilliant. The dashed lines on the star map are the lines you imagine in the sky to help you find other stars.

Orion's Belt

The three stars in the middle of the constellation are called Orion's Belt. They are Mintaka, Alnilam and Alnitak. Just below Orion's Belt is the stellar nursery, the Orion Nebula. This is a fuzzy patch in the sky. If you look closely, you will see a star surrounded by a fuzzy area.

Finding Sirius

From Alnitak imagine a line pointing to the left and downwards and you come to Sirius. Sirius is also known as the Dog Star. Sirius is the most brilliant star in the sky but it is less bright than Venus or Jupiter.

Finding Aldebaran

Imagine a line from Mintaka going upwards and to the right. Carry on past Bellatrix and you will come to Aldebaran.

Finding Procyon and Alphard

If you imagine a line drawn from Bellatrix through Betelgeux then carrying on and curving slightly downwards, you will come to Procyon. This is sometimes called the Little Dog Star. You can continue the line to the left and downwards and you will discover Alphard.

Finding Castor and Pollux

Orion can also help you find the twins, Castor and Pollux. Imagine a line going from Rigel to Betelgeux and then carry on. You will come to the two stars close together that you will recognise as Castor and Pollux. This will help you link the signposts together.

Finding Capella

Capella can also be found from both signposts. Imagine a line going from Saiph to Alnitak and then passing between Betelgeux and Bellatrix and carrying on for quite a long way. Eventually you will come to Capella.

Can you find your way back to the Great Bear?

Did you know?

The largest constellation is Hydra and the smallest is the Southern Cross.

The constellation with the greatest number of bright stars is Orion and the constellation with the fewest visible stars is Mensa.

POLLUX

CASTOR

CAPELLA

ALDEBARAN

PROCYON

BETELGEUX

BELLATRIX

ALPHARD

ALNITAK ALNIDAM

MINTAKA

ORION NEBULA

SAIPH

RIGEL

SIRIUS

Do the constellations move?

The stars seem to swing round the Pole Star during the night. This is because the Earth is spinning. The constellations that are not close to the Pole Star appear to move into and out of the night sky during the year. This is because the Earth is orbiting the Sun.

As the Earth moves round the Sun, we see different parts of space and different constellations, but we can always see the Pole Star and the stars close to it. Just as when you look at opposite walls of your bedroom, you can always look up and see the ceiling.

Circumpolar stars

These are the stars that are visible all year round. In the United Kingdom, the Plough is circumpolar, but we never see the Southern Cross. In the southern hemisphere the Plough can never be seen but the Southern Cross is circumpolar.

Star gazer brolly

To make a star gazer brolly (SGB) you will need an old umbrella and some sticky luminous stars.

Open the umbrella. Think of the centre (where the handle joins the canopy) as the Pole Star. Now stick some of the luminous stars inside the brolly in their correct constellation positions. You can use the maps on pages 29 and 31 to help you.

Hold the SGB above your head and slowly turn it. You can see how the constellations seem to rotate round the handle, or Pole Star. This is how the stars seem to move at night. You can test this for yourself.

Choose a non-cloudy evening in autumn or winter when it gets dark early. Go out and look at the position of the stars at 5.00 p.m. and line up your SGB with them. Fix your SGB securely, then look at the stars again at 8.00 p.m. You will see how much the stars moved. This is because the Earth is spinning.

A star gazer brolly

Star trails are seen in 'time-lapse' photographs because the stars seem to move round the Pole Star during the night

The ten brightest stars

Star	Constellation
Sirius	Canis Major
Canopus	Carina
Alpha Centauri	Centaurus
Arcturus	Bootes
Vega	Lyra
Capella	Auriga
Rigel	Orion
Procyon	Canis Minor
Achernar	Eridanus
Betelgeux	Orion

Pegasus

This picture shows Pegasus the way you'd expect to see a horse, but to see how the stars of this constellation look in the sky, you have to turn this book upside-down. No-one knows why Pegasus is upside-down in the sky.

These are examples of the constellations that can be seen in each season

Searching the sky

Astronomy is the science which deals with the stars and planets. Astronomers study this topic.

Observatories and telescopes

Today, the astronomer's main tool is the telescope. Astronomical telescopes were invented in the early seventeenth century. Observatories are research stations containing telescopes and much other equipment.

There are two main types of light telescope: refractors and reflectors. Refracting telescopes use lenses to collect light, but reflecting telescopes use mirrors to do the same thing. All professional telescopes are now computer-controlled.

On Earth, observatories have to be built well away from cities and bright lights because of light pollution. They are usually found on the tops of mountains where the air is very dark and clear.

The largest telescope on Earth

Living conditions
Because observatories are often in lonely places, astronomers have to make sure they have enough food and drink and somewhere to sleep.

The world's largest mirror telescope is the Keck telescope in Hawaii. It has a mirror 10 metres across. The Hubble Space Telescope is not the largest, but it is in the best place – in space orbiting the Earth and well away from bright lights.

Light pollution

The full moon provides useful light during the night. Astronomers often get annoyed with the presence of the full moon because the light drowns the faint light of the stars, making them difficult to see. This is a natural form of light pollution.

Artificial light is a much bigger problem for astronomers. Cities and towns keep getting bigger. There are industrial centres and shopping centres with more and more street lights. People who live in large cities or near large shopping centres find it very difficult to see any stars at all.

From space you can see where all the major centres of industry and population are by the amount of light. It looks very impressive.

Providing adequate light at night is very important so people can see where they are going and be safe. However, if street lights were designed to direct all their light downwards, then less energy would be used. This would be good for everyone because roads and paths would be brightly lit and the night sky would remain dark.

The Hubble Space Telescope being launched from the space shuttle

See for yourself

Next time you are in a car or on a train at night, look at the glow of the lights above the towns and cities. This is light pollution.

City lights in the British Isles seen from space at night

Space travel

Space travel to explore the Solar System and beyond, means very long journeys. It is important to learn how to live and work in space for very long periods of time; at least a year and probably longer.

Since the 1970s, the Americans and Russians have launched space stations which orbit the Earth and allow astronauts to work in space. A new multi-national space station is likely to be put in space next century.

Inside the spacecraft

Working and living conditions in space are very different from those on the Earth. In space there is no air or gravity. Astronauts can take their own air with them, but they cannot take gravity. In space, astronauts float around their spacecraft rather than walk around it.

Scientists have tried to make life as normal as possible for the astronauts. Inside the spacecraft, astronauts wear their normal space clothes. They eat their food from a tray using a knife and fork, but drinking has to be done from a special bottle with a stem.

Going to the lavatory is very different in space. Waste material in the lavatory doesn't fall down the bowl. It has to be sucked away by air. And astronauts have to wear a seat belt to stop them from floating away.

Casual clothes are not very different in space ...

What happens to water
It is important not to have water droplets floating around a spacecraft because without gravity the droplets will eventually run together and form one big 'floating lake'.

... but playing an instrument is

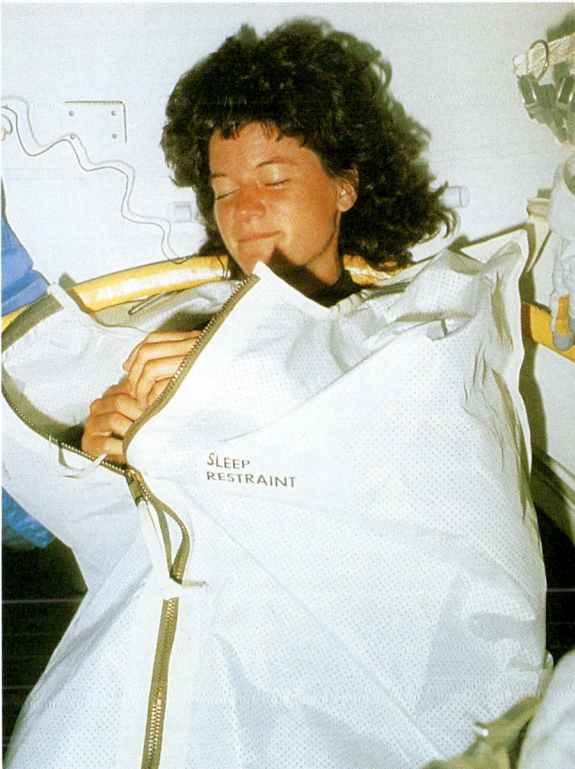

Astronauts sleep zipped into sleeping bags that are attached to the floor or wall. If they are not fastened down, the astronauts could drift across the cabin and possibly injure themselves.

Out in space

Outside the spacecraft, astronauts must wear spacesuits. Spacesuits protect the astronaut from harmful cosmic rays; they also have air tanks attached to them for the astronaut to breathe.

To work outside, astronauts may use a manned manoeuvring unit (MMU) – a sort of flying armchair that allows them to move away from the spacecraft. The MMU is moved by firing little jets of gas out of the backpack, like mini rockets.

You have to sleep strapped down...

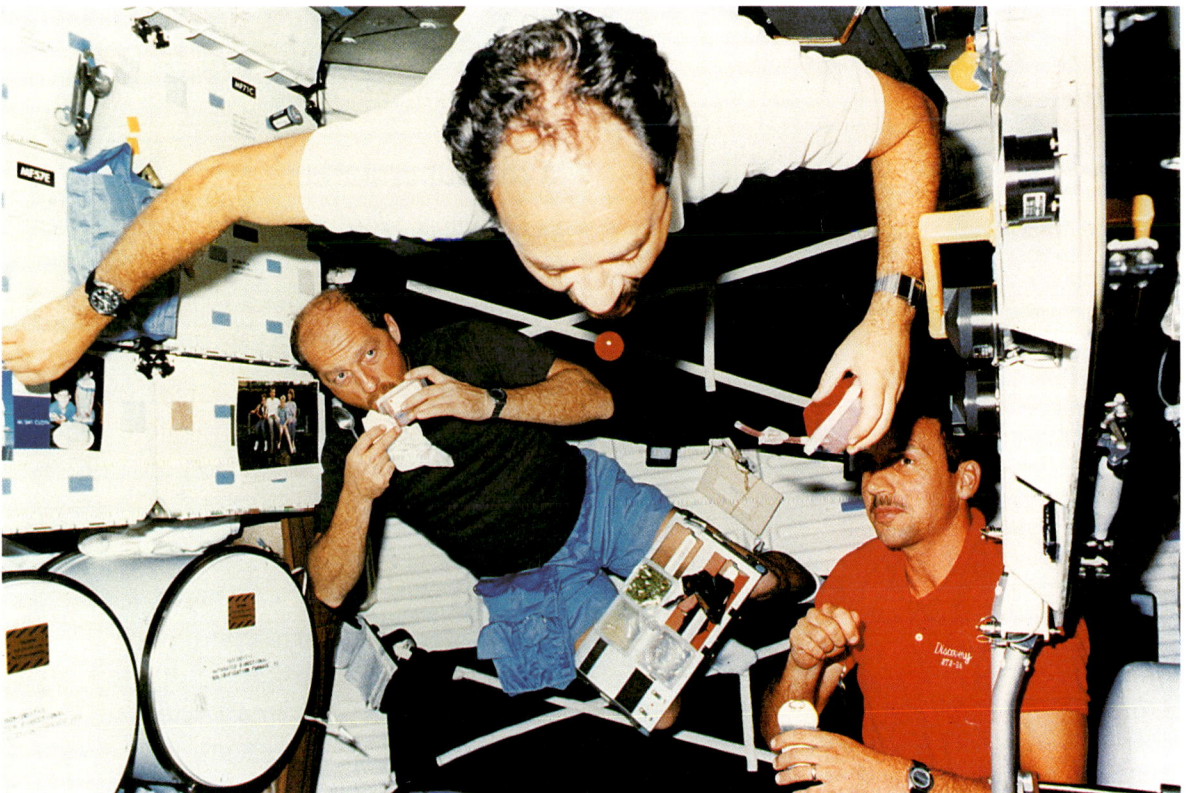

... but drink might float free

Spin-offs from space

Space technology affects our life today in all sorts of ways.

In the home

One of the first materials to be developed for use in space was Teflon. Nothing sticks to it and it is now used for non-stick frying pans.

Tools such as cordless drills were originally developed because astronauts working in space required tools that had their own power sources. After all, they couldn't plug a tool into an electric socket in space.

Solid lubricants were also developed for use in space. The most famous one is WD–40. Many people spray this onto their car engines to help them start.

In the supermarket

Sandwiches are often sold in a clear plastic triangular wrapper. This packaging was originally developed to keep food fresh for the astronauts in the 1960s.

Plastic thinly coated with metal was also developed in the 1960s as insulation material. Today, it is found as wrappers for crisps and sweets.

There are millions of parts in a space shuttle. Every part is numbered electronically so that a computer can read its number. Supermarkets and shops use this technology to keep a check on their stock. You know the system used – it is the bar code you see on anything you buy from a supermarket.

ISBN 0-563-37567-1

9 780563 375678 >

Clothes

Mylar is another insulating material used in space exploration. Now you can find it in sleeping bags and outdoor jackets. Ambulance paramedics use Mylar blankets to keep injured people warm until they get to hospital.

To help astronauts train for weightless conditions, training shoes with pockets of air in their soles were developed in the mid-1980s. Many sports shoes now have this type of sole.

In the workplace

A lap-top computer is a small portable computer. These were developed in the 1980s because astronauts are very busy in space and do not have the time to keep going back to the main computer. They need a small computer that can be carried around.

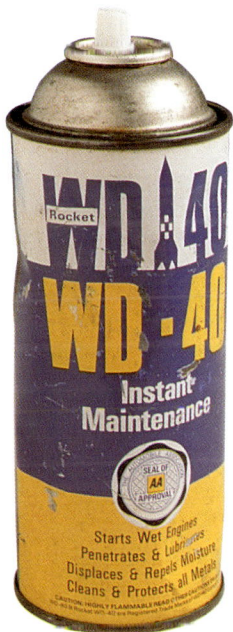

Extra info

Velcro was invented long before the space programme but it was used in the 1960s in the Gemini and Apollo spacecraft. It lined the walls of the spacecraft so astronauts could stick things onto it to prevent them floating away.

Is anybody there?

We do not know if there is any other life in the Universe. We are certain there is no other life in the Solar System. The planets closer than Earth to the Sun are too hot; those further away are too cold.

Mars is the planet that most resembles Earth. In 1976, two spacecraft landed on Mars to look for life. They did not find any but they did send back photographs from the Martian surface. Today, it looks dry and bleak and is cold. We don't know if microbe life forms existed there when a thick atmosphere and water were present. We will have to wait until manned missions visit Mars to find the answer.

The Universe is huge

The Solar System is a tiny region of space ruled by the Sun. Our Sun is one of about 100 000 million stars that make up our galaxy, the Milky Way. It is a spiral galaxy. There are millions of galaxies in the Universe. The Milky Way is neither the largest nor the smallest.

In the southern hemisphere it is possible to see some nearby galaxies. They are called the Large Magellanic Cloud and the Small Magellanic Cloud. They were first observed by Ferdinand Magellan who sailed round the world in 1519–21.

On a very clear night it is possible to see the constellation Andromeda and a small 'fuzzy' area in space. This is the Andromeda galaxy; it is 2.2 million light years away. It is the most distant object you can see without a telescope or binoculars.

The Large Magellanic Cloud can only be seen from the southern hemisphere

The radio telescope at Jodrell Bank looks for messages from space

We imagine all kinds of other life forms

The ten closest stars to us

Star	Distance in light years
Proxima Centauri	4.2
Alpha Centauri A	4.3
Alpha Centauri B	4.3
Barnard's Star	6.0
Wolf 359	7.7
BD + 36° 2147	8.2
Sirius A	8.6
Sirius B	8.6
UV Ceti A	8.9
UV Ceti B	8.9

Looking for life

Project SETI (Search for Extraterrestrial Intelligence) uses powerful radio telescopes to look for messages from space, but so far, there have not been any.

Space probes have been sent into deep space beyond the Solar System. These spacecraft carry messages that might be found by another intelligent civilisation.

The speed of light

Light travels extremely fast but the Universe is so big that it can take years for light from a star to reach us. A light year is the distance travelled by light in one year; it is about 9.5 million million km or 6 million million miles.

Astronomy logbook

BC

2500
Astronomical
records begin

585
An eclipse of
the Sun is first
predicted

350
Aristotle
suggests the
Earth is round

240
The size of
the Earth is
estimated

140
The first star
catalogue is
drawn

1957
Sputnik 1 is the first
artificial satellite

1959
The first photograph
of the far side of the
Moon is taken

1961
Yuri Gagarin is the
first man in space

1962
Mariner 2 to Venus is
the first successful
probe to another planet

1963
Valentina Tereshkova is
the first woman in space

1969
Neil Armstrong and
Buzz Aldrin are the first
men on the Moon

1976
Viking 1 and 2
land on Mars

AD

813
The Baghdad
School of
Astronomy is
founded

1543
Copernicus says
the Earth is not
the centre of the
Universe

1610
Galileo uses the
first astronomical
telescope

1675
The Royal Greenwich
Observatory is founded

1781
Uranus is
discovered

1801
The first
asteroid is
discovered

1840
The first photograph
of the Moon is taken

1846
Neptune is
discovered

1930
Pluto is
discovered

1981
The space shuttle
is tested

1990
The Hubble Space
Telescope is launched

1991
The Keck telescope
is built – it is the
largest in the world

1994
Comet Shoemaker/Levy 9
smashes into Jupiter

The Zodiac

The ancient astronomers noticed that the five bright planets they could see were only ever seen in the same part of the sky as certain constellations. These constellations are in a band across the sky. The path that the Sun appears to travel during the day is in the same band. This band is called the Zodiac.

Zodiac means 'circle of animals'. It is the name for the collection of constellations where the planets are seen during an Earth year. They are mostly named after animals. The Zodiac was discovered by the ancient astronomers and is now used by astrologers. Astronomers study the stars as a science. Astrologers think that your life is affected by the positions of the planets and the stars and the Sun when you were born.

There are thirteen constellations in the Zodiac. Twelve of them are the ones whose names appear as the signs of the zodiac or star signs in newspapers and magazines. The extra one is called Ophiuchus, the Serpent Bearer. It is found between Scorpius and Sagittarius.

The planets Mercury and Pluto have orbits that sometimes take them out of the main band of the Zodiac. These planets can sometimes be seen in other constellations.

Do you know all the constellations in the zodiac?

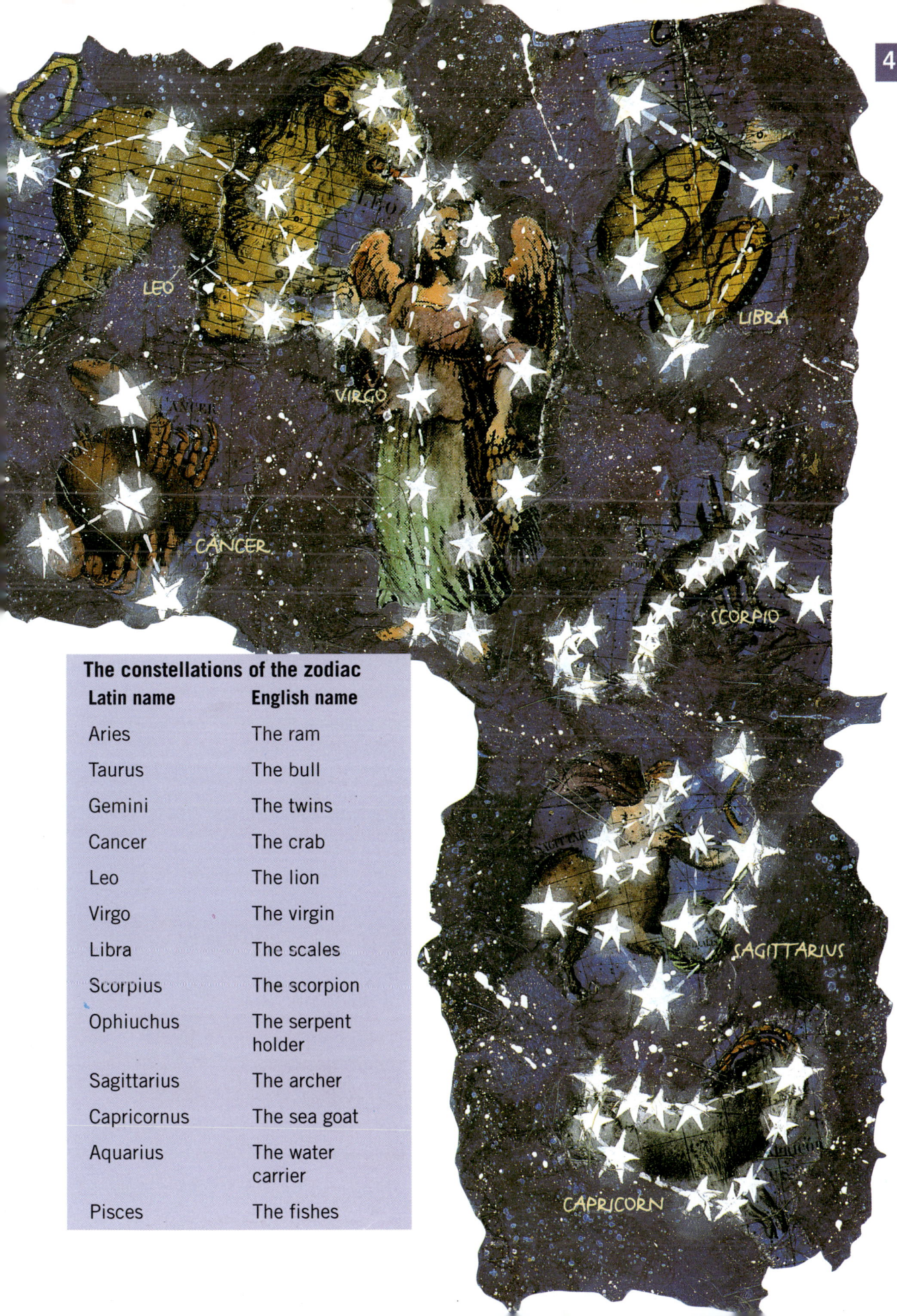

The constellations of the zodiac

Latin name	English name
Aries	The ram
Taurus	The bull
Gemini	The twins
Cancer	The crab
Leo	The lion
Virgo	The virgin
Libra	The scales
Scorpius	The scorpion
Ophiuchus	The serpent holder
Sagittarius	The archer
Capricornus	The sea goat
Aquarius	The water carrier
Pisces	The fishes

Glossary

Astronomy   The science dealing with stars and planets

Atmosphere   The layers of gas surrounding a planet

Circumpolar star   A star which circles the Pole Star

Comet   A 'dirty snowball' made of rock, and dust in ice

Constellation   A pattern or group of stars

Day   The period taken by a planet to spin once on its axis

Eclipse (lunar)   The time when the Moon passes into the shadow cast by the Earth

Eclipse (solar)   The time when the Moon passes in front of the Sun

Galaxies   Star systems with thousands of millions of stars

Gnomon   The pointer of a sundial

Halley's Comet   The only bright comet whose return can be predicted; it returns to the Sun every 76 years

Light year   The distance travelled by light in one year; it is equal to about 9.5 million million kilometres or 6 million million miles

Meteor   A tiny particle in space that burns up when it dashes into the Earth's atmosphere and produces a shooting star

Meteorite   A rock large enough to survive burning up in the atmosphere and that may produce a crater when it falls to Earth

Midnight sun   The Sun seen above the horizon at midnight during summer within the Arctic or Antarctic Circle

Observatory   An astronomical research station

Orbit   The path of a planet, satellite or asteroid

Phases of the Moon   The apparent changes in shape of the Moon

Planets   The most important members of the Solar System apart from the Sun

Plough   The nickname for Ursa Major, the Great Bear

Polaris   The Pole Star

Proxima Centauri   The nearest star beyond the Sun

Seasons   Differences in weather and temperature due to the tilt of the Earth as it orbits the Sun

Shooting star   The popular name for a meteor

Solar System   The system made up of the Sun, planets, satellites, comets, asteroids, meteorites, dust and gas

Star   A gaseous body that produces its own light (also called a sun)

Sundial   An instrument used to tell the time by using a pole or rod (the gnomon) to cast a shadow on a scale

Telescope   The main instrument used to see stars and planets

The Moon   The Earth's satellite

The Sun   The star which is the central body of the Solar System

Year   The time taken for a planet to go once round the Sun

Zodiac   A band of constellations stretching around the sky and in which the planets are seen

This is what our planet looks like from space, you can see the British Isles

Published by BBC Educational Publishing, a division of BBC Education, BBC White City, 201 Wood Lane, London W12 7TS

First published in this form 1997
© Martin Lunn/BBC Education 1995
The moral right of the author has been asserted.

Colour reproduction by Dot Gradations Ltd, U.K.

Acknowledgements

Edited by Penelope Lyons
Designed by Charlotte Crace
Picture research by Helen Taylor

Illustrations: © Brigid Collins 1995 (pages 29, 31, 33, 42-3 and 44-5); © Line & Line 1995 (pages 5, 6, 9, 22 and 26); © The Maltings Partnership 1995 (pages 4, 8, 13 (top) and 24-5); © Steve Noon 1995 (pages 11, 13 (bottom), 14 and 32)

Photos: Bridgeman Art Library/Giraudon **p. 2 (top)**; Andrew Cottam **p. 12;** Mary Evans Picture Library **p. 27 (top);** Luke Finn/BBC Education **pp. 38/39;** Akira Fujii **p. 27 (bottom);** The Garden Picture Library **p. 4;** Images Colour Library **p. 3;** Kobal Collection **p. 41 (right);** NASA **pp. 10 (bottom), 11, 17 (bottom), 19 (top), 36 (left), 37 (bottom);** Science Photo Library **pp. 2 (bottom), 5, 7 (bottom), 9, 10 (top), 14, 15 (top), 16, 17 (top and middle), 19 (middle and bottom), 20, 21, 23, 33, 34, 35, 36 (right), 37 (top), 40, 41 (left), 47;** Roger W. Sinnott **p. 15 (bottom);** Staatliche Kunstsammlungen, Dresden **p. 7 (top)** detail from *The Kingdom of Flora* by Nicholas Poussin

ENVIRONMENT

Written by

Keith Bishop

Illustrated by

Maltings Partnership, Satchel Illustration
and Cathy Morley

CONTENTS

The global environment

This book is about the environment – the environment we share with other people and with millions of different species of plants and animals. It explores how we change and damage the environment as a result of our actions.

There are many problems that are endangering the future of this planet. Most of these problems are linked with one another. However, people have different opinions about how science can help us solve them.

The highlighted words on these pages will give you a guide to these links. Turn to the glossary on page 46 to see what they mean. This will help you to see some of the major environmental issues and how they are linked.

The Sun – sunlight and warmth travelling 150 million km is the source of energy for life on Earth.

Biosphere

This is the living land, air and water around the Earth which supports plant and animal life.

Global warming

This is a problem of too much carbon dioxide and other **greenhouse gases**. These gases cause too much of the Sun's energy to be trapped in the biosphere.

Acid rain

Fossil fuels release toxic gases that cause **acid rain** when they are burnt to make electricity.

Alternative energy sources

These offer other ways of making electricity, but they have their problems.

Holes in the sky

The **ozone layer** is a natural filter that blocks out most of the dangerous ultra-violet rays from the Sun. The man-made **CFCs** that destroy the ozone layer are also greenhouse gases.

Rainforests

The rainforests pump oxygen into the biosphere and also reduce the amount of carbon dioxide. Cutting down and burning the forests simply increases the level of greenhouse gases and that leads to **global warming**.

Endangered species

Fifty per cent of the world's species of plants and animals live in the rainforests. If we destroy the rainforests, we reduce the natural **biodiversity** of the planet.

Stratosphere

Troposphere

The Earth

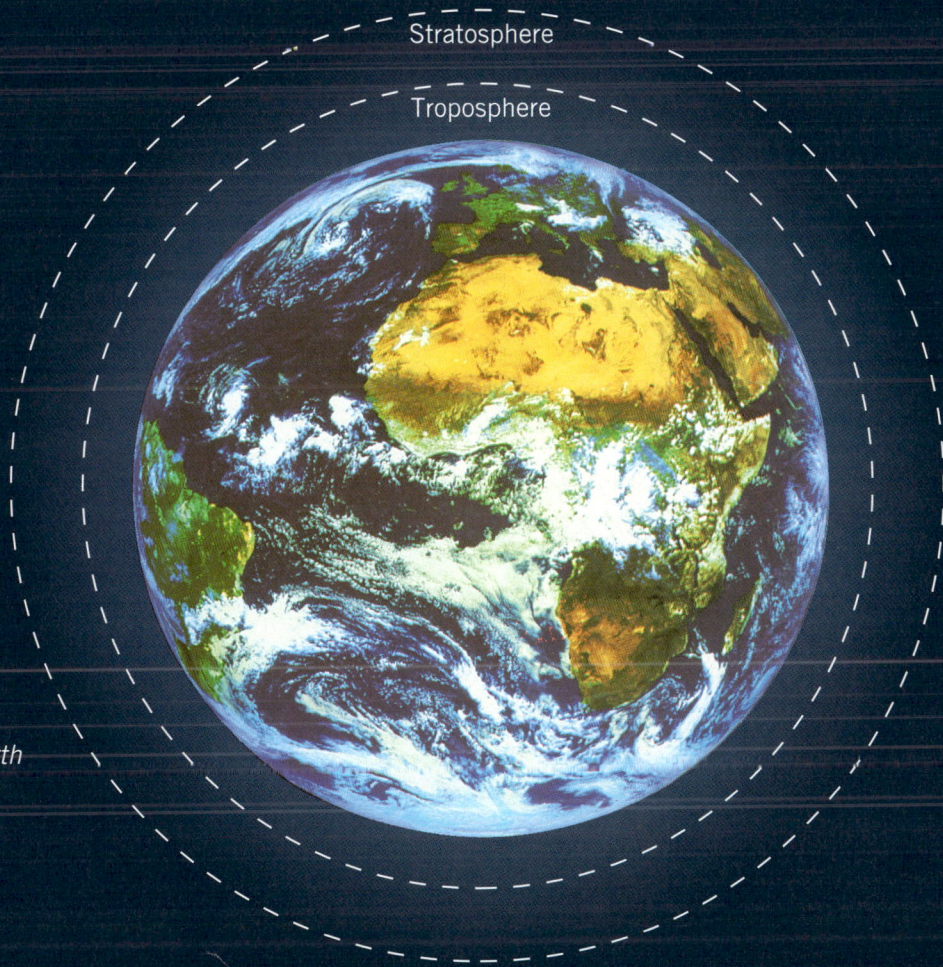

Deserting the Earth

Deforestation and over-grazing take away the soil's natural protective layer of plants. The result is poor quality soil. This process is called **desertification**.

Mountains of waste

Non-renewable resources are wasted to produce rubbish which then **pollutes** the environment. Tipping rubbish in landfill sites or burning it produces greenhouse gases, and **pollutes** the water supply.

Radioactive waste

This does not give off greenhouse gases or gases that cause acid rain. However, radioactive waste is a long term pollutant which nobody wants and which is difficult to get rid of.

Fresh water

Global warming could be affecting the pattern of rainfall around the globe. **Pollution** of the water supply is caused by sewage and **toxins** from domestic waste.

Seaworld

Toxins and other pollutants from industry damage the **food chains** in the sea.

Transport today

Transport is using up non-renewable resources and polluting the atmosphere with greenhouse gases and other toxins.

Transport tomorrow

Transport of the future will have a major impact on global warming and the health of the environment.

Agenda 21

In June 1992, in Rio de Janeiro, 35 000 people attended the biggest conference ever held in the world – the Earth Summit. Representatives from 178 countries were there to talk about the environment. It produced a report called Agenda 21 which presented 115 proposals about sustainable living from now into the 21st Century.

Children with 'The tree of life' at the Earth Summit, Rio de Janeiro, Brazil

The Earth Summit also produced two important agreements about climate change and biodiversity.

1 Climate change

This says that, by the year 2000, emissions of carbon dioxide and other greenhouse gases must be cut back to 1990 levels.

2 Biodiversity

This aims to protect plant and animal species all over the world before it's too late.

These two agreements might seem simple enough, but actually achieving them is not going to be so easy. If we are going to have an environment healthy enough to sustain future generations, then governments must agree to act now.

What did the Earth Summit achieve?

The Earth Summit brought people from all over the world to talk together. They produced Agenda 21 – a 600 billion dollar action programme to save the planet. Agenda 21 asks how you want to see the planet being treated and what kind of future you want to see for your children and grandchildren. Most of Agenda 21 says what governments can do, but there is a chapter aimed at young people and how important their involvement is.

Local Agenda 21

Agenda 21 can can only work if people act locally. Local Agenda 21 is your chance to be involved in environmental action and find ways to 'be more sustainable' in your local area.

In England and Wales, every local council is expected to organise a Local Agenda 21 to bring people together to act on environmental issues. Most councils have a Environmental Services Department which deals with environmental issues such as conservation or recycling.

How can I be involved?

You can find out what is going on in your area by ringing the council number and asking for information about Local Agenda 21. Solutions to local problems can have a knock-on effect which will improve the global environment. Local Agenda 21 will help you make those links between local and global problems.

Local Agenda 21 can put you in touch with community groups and help you to meet other people who want to do something for their environment. If there aren't any groups, then it could help you form groups and advise you what to do.

They may also be able to provide some funds to help you get started when you know what you want to do.

What can we do?

Here are some ideas for Local Agenda 21 action:

■ Find out how you could help to reduce traffic pollution in your area.

■ Develop a community composting project.

■ Repair local footpaths.

■ Increase biodiversity. Develop green spaces as conservation areas.

■ Clean up a local pond or stream. Set up a study to find out where the pollution is coming from.

■ Write to your local MP about any issues that concern you.

Local Agenda 21 is about meeting other people in your community to take action on the environment.

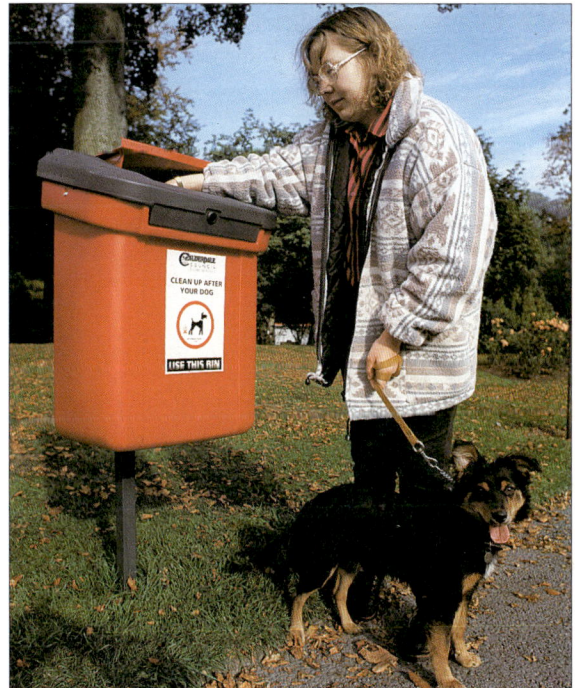

Dog mess bins encourage people to keep their environment clean and safe.

Sustainable living

Sustainable living is about caring for the Earth and its systems for supporting life. It's about whether we can go on damaging the environment for future generations by using up the Earth's resources and polluting the environment with waste.

Have you ever thought about all the rubbish that's left at the end of a party? Someone comes round and sweeps all the the clingfilm, plastic cups, spoons, knives, forks and paper plates into a big, black, plastic bin liner. Think about how long this material was used for before it was thrown away. Where did it all come from, and where is it all going to end up?

The plastics all come from oil which is a non-renewable resource. When it's used up, it can't be replaced. Why do we treat the Earth's resources in this way? We use them up when we make things, only to throw them away again almost as quickly.

Are we misusing our natural resources by always making 'throwaway' things? In other words, is our style of living sustainable? Will there still be enough resources left for future generations?

These are all examples of 'throwaway' goods. Can you think of some more examples?

By the year 2030, the population in the developing world will have doubled. But it will take over a hundred years for the population to double in the developed world.

N
W—E
S

RUSSIA

NORTH AMERICA

EUROPE

ASIA

developed

SOUTH AMERICA

AFRICA

developing

no data

AUSTRALIA

80%

80%

65%

35%

20%

20%

2 billion

3.5 billion

Resources used

Energy used

Cars (500 million)

Population (1995)

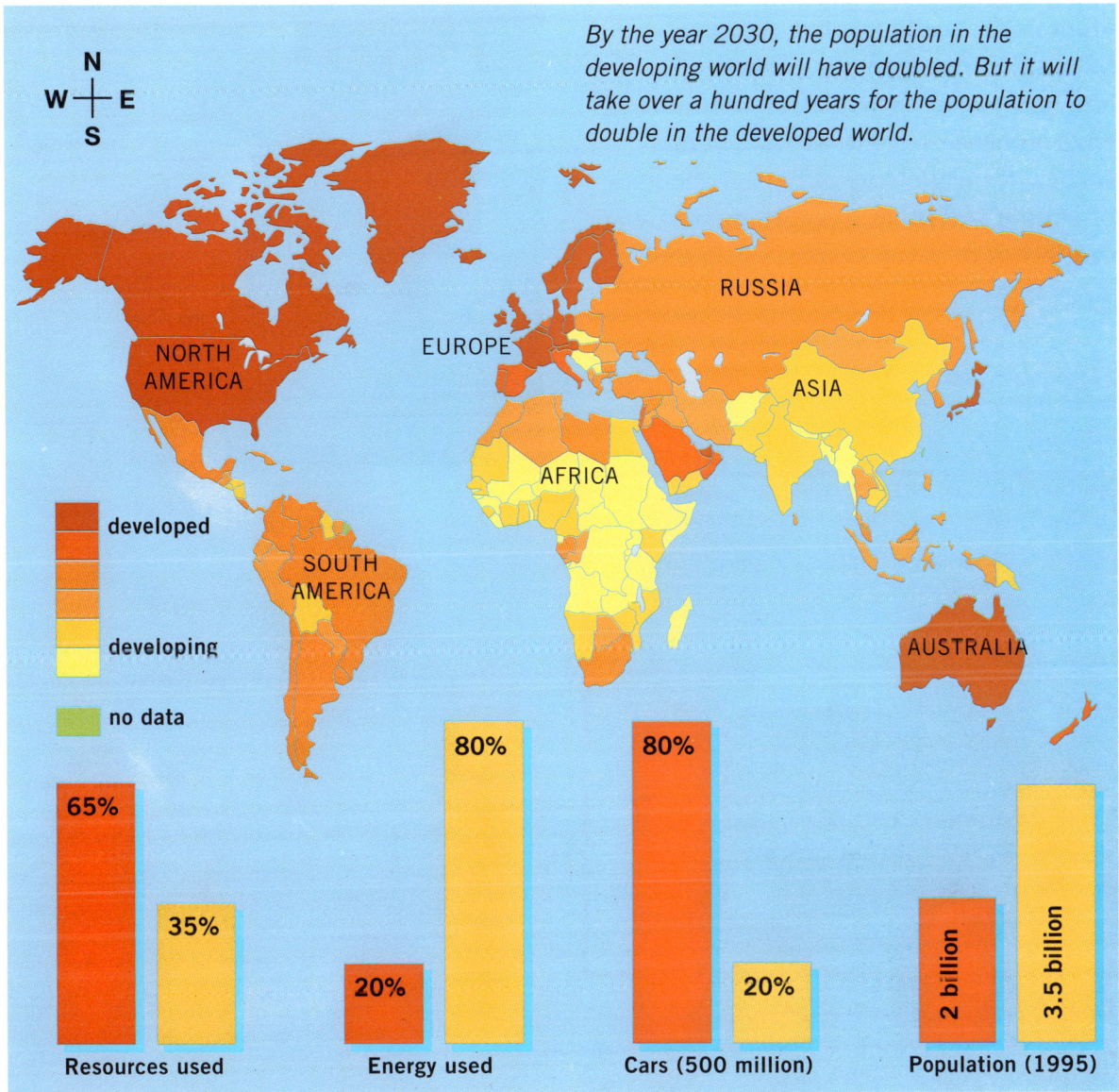

Who's using up the resources?

The developed world has a quarter of the world's population, but it uses up twice the amount of resources as the other three quarters (see map above).

Look at the map and work out roughly what the world population could be by the year 2030. Where do you think most of the new people on the planet will be living?

Damaging the environment

High living standards means using the Earth's resources to make consumer goods like toys, cars, televisions and washing machines. But making the goods, as well as using them and then throwing them away, creates waste. And waste can cause pollution which damages the environment.

Think about what will happen to the environment if everyone lives this way.

Global links

Human beings do not live separately from other living things. We are all linked together through our common environment. Actions we take in our corner of the globe could affect the lives of people and other living things thousands of miles away.

CFCs destroy the ozone layer high in the atmosphere.

Growing cash crops, such as peanuts, reduces the amount of land available for people to graze their animals and grow their own food.

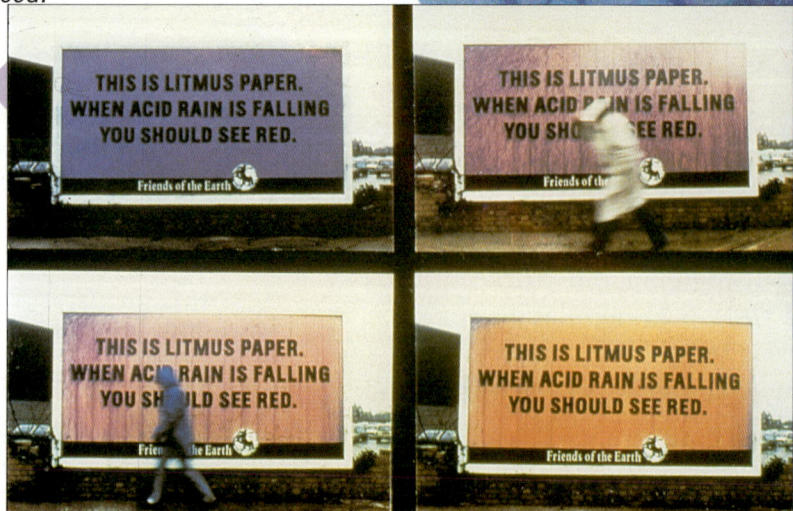

THIS IS LITMUS PAPER. WHEN ACID RAIN IS FALLING YOU SHOULD SEE RED.

Friends of the Earth

Acid rain is pollution which falls wherever the wind blows it.

Doctors claim that traffic fumes increase the chances of children becoming asthmatic.

Endangered species are threatened by people who want to buy their skins, tusks or other parts of their bodies.

Scientists are sure that increasing carbon dioxide levels are causing the climate to change all round the world.

The global greenhouse

Have you ever walked into a greenhouse on a cool but bright, sunny day? It feels nice and warm. In fact, we all live in a global greenhouse. The Earth's atmosphere acts just like the glass and keeps the warmth in. Without this 'greenhouse effect', life could not exist as we know it. Our worry now is that the Earth is getting a bit too warm, and we're not sure what the consequences might be.

Global warming

This increased greenhouse effect is called global warming. It is caused by too much carbon dioxide in the air. Carbon dioxide is the most important of the greenhouse gases simply because some of us produce so much of it. A person in the United States, for example, causes emissions of carbon dioxide ten times more than someone in Asia.

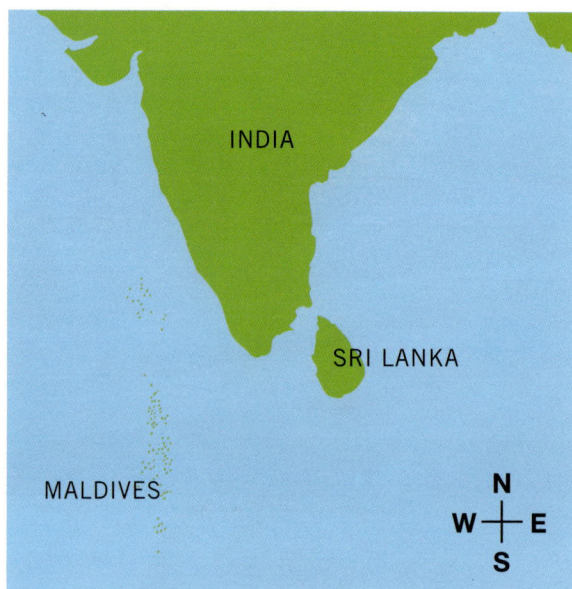

The highest point on the Maldives Islands is only 160 cm above sea level.

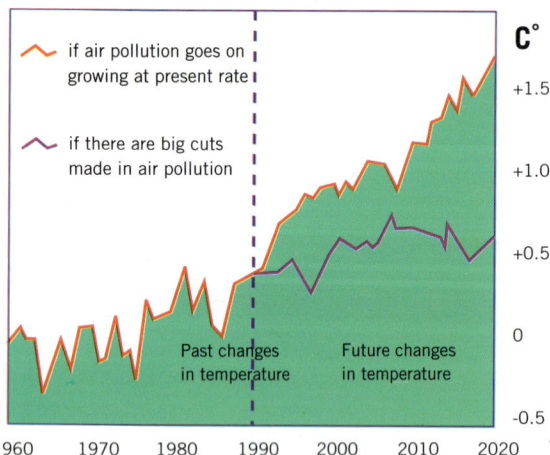

What's the problem?

The average temperature of the sea and the atmosphere is going up. By the year 2030, it could be 1 degree higher. This doesn't seem much, but it could be enough to start melting the polar ice caps. It's estimated that 2.5 thousand square miles of the ice shelf in Antarctica has already disappeared into the sea during the last fifty years. If this is true, the sea level will rise. You may not worry too much about flooding if you live well above sea level, but millions of people don't! Look at the map. The Maldives Islands could disappear under water completely.

We are also worried about changing weather patterns. Many countries already suffer from low rainfall. Global warming could make matters worse by causing even more severe droughts.

Where's all the carbon dioxide coming from?

Industrialised countries burn massive amounts of fossil fuel to make electricity and to provide fuel for transport.

It's estimated that an average British family is responsible for 20 tonnes of carbon dioxide being pumped into the air every year. In the 1990s, this adds up world wide to about 500 billion tonnes a year.

dioxide back into the atmosphere. Unless we replant trees, there will be fewer and fewer to use up the carbon dioxide.

Carbon dioxide isn't the only greenhouse gas that's causing the problem. There are others such as CFCs (see page 14) from fridges, and even methane gas from animal pits on farms!

A burning rainforest in the Amazon

Greenhouse gases

Not only do trees use up carbon dioxide when they photosynthesise but when they are burnt (see photo), they release carbon

What can we do?

The Earth Summit (see page 52) produced a very important agreement called the Law on Climate Change. This says that, by the year 2000, countries should reduce their carbon dioxide emissions to the 1990 level. This is a real challenge if developing countries are also going to improve their living standards at the same time.

What can you do? Look at the pictures (below) to give you some ideas of how you can help reduce greenhouse gases.

Simple actions can help to reduce greenhouse gases. Every little helps!

Acid rain

Waste gases from power stations, industry and transport rise high into the sky and pollute the atmosphere. There they travel with the wind, often over vast distances, crossing different countries as they go. The gases dissolve in water in the clouds and fall back to the Earth as acid rain. This causes environmental damage.

All European countries produce acid rain by releasing poisonous gases which pollute the atmosphere. Look at the map. Which countries do you think are going to suffer most from acid rain?

Which gases make acid rain?

There are two main gases: sulphur dioxide (SO_2) and nitrogen oxides (NO_x).

The sulphur dioxide comes mostly from coal-fired power stations and heavy industry. Most of the nitrogen oxides come from the exhaust gases of cars and trucks.

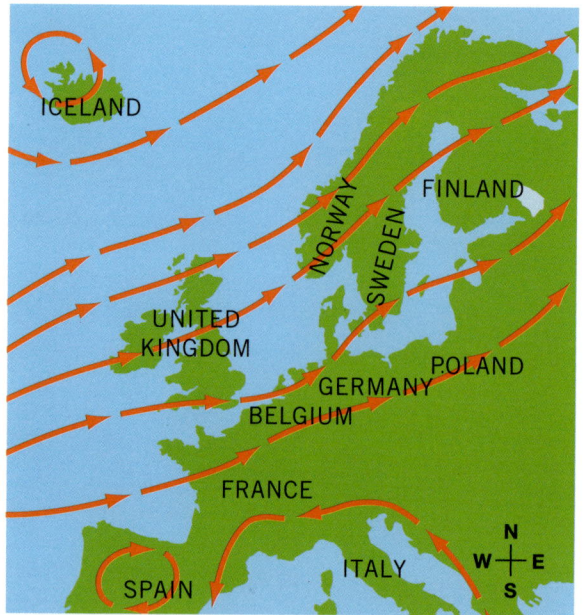

Prevailing winds blow from the south west and take pollution over Scandinavia.

Key
- coal with sulphur impurities
- coal burnt in power station
- SO_2 drifts into atmosphere
- SO_2 combines with water
- acid rain falls to Earth
- exhaust gases containing NO_x and SO_2

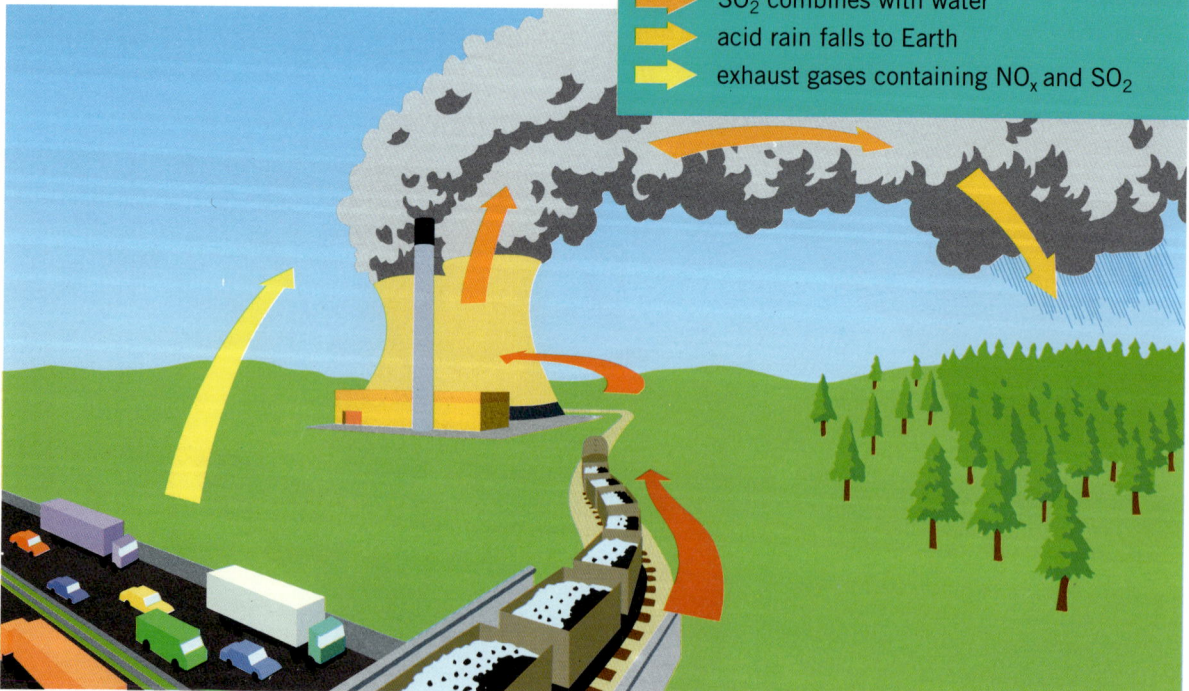

What could be done to reduce the amount of acid rain being formed?

What's the damage?

Acid rain gets into the soil and affects the way trees grow. The branches begin to sag and die back.

Acid rain damage to a statue in Poland. What do you feel about the damage acid rain does?

Many beautiful buildings and statues, particularly those made from limestone or marble, are dissolved away by acid rain (see photo).

Acid rain also pollutes freshwater lakes. Over 40 per cent of Sweden's lakes are now almost lifeless. The photo (below) shows a beautiful, crystal clear lake. If you looked closely, you would see very few plants or fish. This is because the water is too acidic for living things to survive.

The polluter pays

Together, the United States and Europe release over 70 million tons of sulphur dioxide and 40 million tonnes of nitrogen oxides into the atmosphere every year. They are responsible for 80 per cent of the world's acid rain and photochemical smog.

Some people think that if you pollute the environment, then you should pay for the damage you cause. This is called 'the polluter pays' principle. What do you think of this idea?

Lake Gardsjon, Sweden. This lake is polluted by acid rain. Only the very hardiest plants and animals can survive in the water.

What can we do?

Acid rain is a problem that can be controlled. Coal-fired power stations can be fitted with sulphur dioxide removers, but they are expensive.

Another suggestion is that we should build nuclear power stations, or gas-fired power stations instead of burning coal (see page 73).

What can you do? You could help to reduce acid rain pollution by using less electricity and by using the car less often (see pages 85 and 91).

Holes in the sky

High in the sky, over 10 kilometres above the surface, a thin protective blanket of gas surrounds the Earth. This is the ozone layer, a natural sunblock which filters out the Sun's harmful ultra-violet rays. But during the last twenty years, a large hole has been discovered over the South Pole. Fortunately, not many people live below the hole, but if we don't look after the atmosphere it could be dangerous for people living nearby.

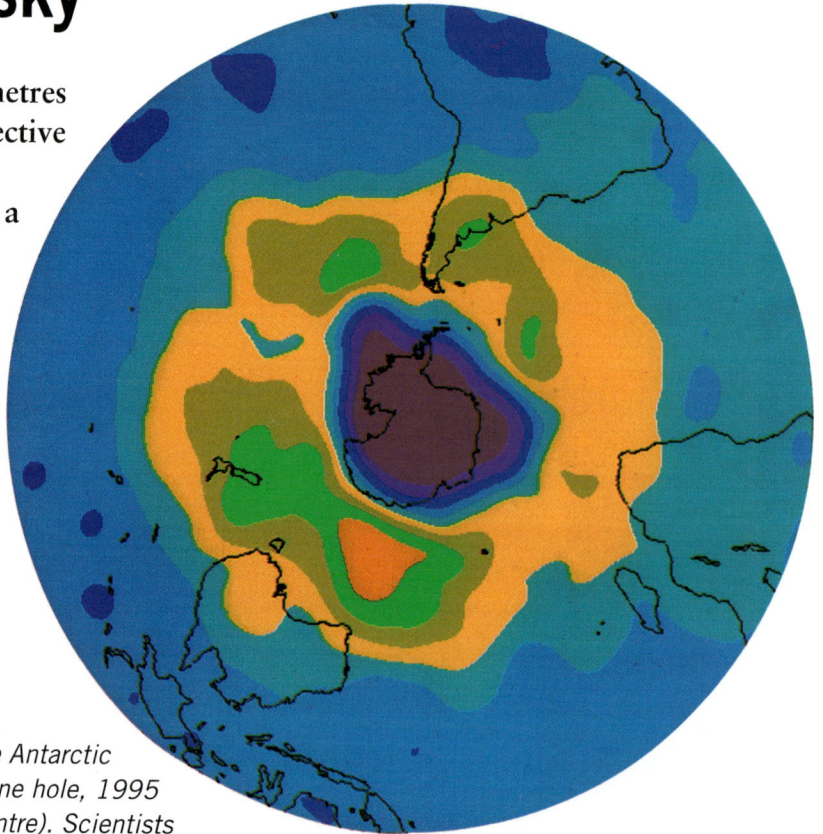

The Antarctic ozone hole, 1995 (centre). Scientists say that the hole is getting bigger each year.

CFCs are used to make these products

CFCs

The holes are where the ozone has thinned to almost a third of what it should be. The cause is mainly a group of chemicals, known as CFCs (chlorofluorocarbons). We use these CFCs to make products such as fridges, foam packaging and fire extinguishers.

We used CFCs because we had no idea what damage they would do. No one realised they would drift up into the stratosphere and set off reactions which would break up the ozone into oxygen.

Unless we do something about the release of CFCs into the environment, our fear is that these holes will gradually grow bigger each year.

Dangerous holes

You've probably been warned lots of times about the dangers of sunbathing. People don't realise that the ultra-violet rays damage living cells and this can sometimes cause skin cancer – even ten to twenty years later.

It is important not to expose your skin to the sun for long periods of time. Try to wear a hat and always use lotions with high protection levels (SPF 15–25).

Banning CFCs

In 1987, governments around the world got together in Montreal. They agreed to ban CFCs and other ozone depleting substances (ODSs) by the year 2000. This was called the Montreal Protocol. Since then, industry has been producing a safer alternative called HFCs. Unfortunately some countries are still producing CFCs, and CFCs are still being sold illegally in the United States.

Did you realise over 100 000 people die every year from skin cancer (melanoma)?

What can we do?

The Montreal Protocol is helping to limit the damage, but the use of CFCs must be stopped. We have no idea what the consequences might be for future generations.

What can you do? If you live in a country where CFCs are still used, you can help by checking that any product you buy is 'CFC free'.

If your family buys a new fridge, make sure that the old one is properly recycled. Check with your local council on how to dispose of it safely.

Some fast food companies use polystyrene containers for their products. Write and ask them if these containers were made using CFCs.

OZONE FRIENDLY

Rainforests

Rainforests are hot, steamy environments where the rainfall can reach 200 mm in a year. They are rich in a wonderful variety of plants and animals, many of which have yet to be discovered. They are also the source of over a quarter of the Earth's oxygen supply. Agenda 21 says they are disappearing so fast that, at this rate, they could all be gone by the year 2035.

Whose rainforest is it?

The native people who live in the rainforest would say it's theirs. But their governments see the rainforest as a way of earning money quickly.

Native people understand the rainforest in a way that we don't. They have developed a sustainable way of life where they take no more from the forest than the forest can replace.

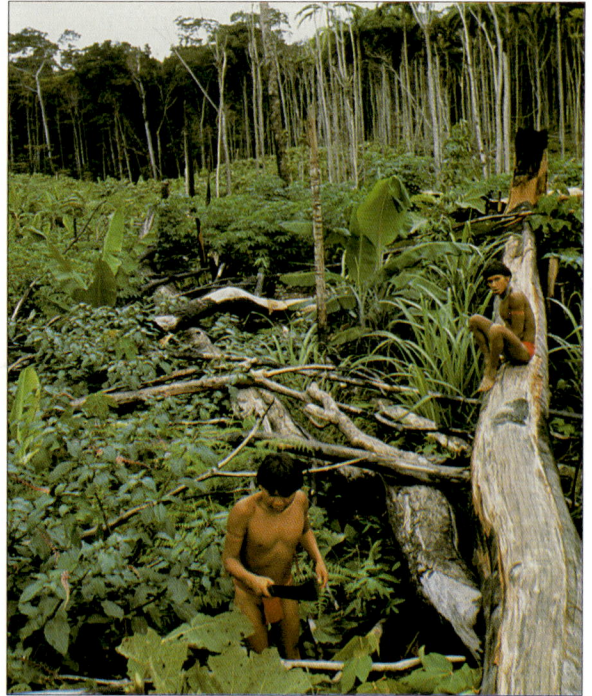

The Yanomami tribe, Venezuelan rainforest. There are over 300 million tribal people in the world.

In which parts of the world are rainforests mostly found?

Destroying the rainforest

There are many different reasons for rainforest destruction. The pie chart will help you see how rainforests are being destroyed. The reasons are mostly to do with earning money.

1 Logging destroys most of the forest. Teak, mahogany and ebony are highly prized hardwoods used for making furniture. They take hundreds of years to grow.

2 Ranching also destroys the forest. Much of the beef for burgers in America comes from cattle ranches where there used to be rainforest.

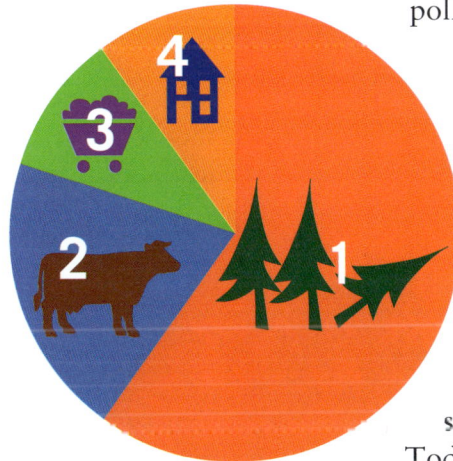

Logging in Queensland, Australia

3 Mining is another reason. Many rainforests are rich in minerals containing silver, copper and gold. Trees are cleared to mine the minerals, leading to soil erosion and landslides. The process of extracting minerals creates terrible pollution of the rivers.

4 Workers from other areas come to work in the rainforest which is burned and cleared to build homes. Few of these workers are the native people.

Twenty years ago, Australia had 200 000 square miles of rainforest. Today, this is down to 60 000 square miles. Logging is the major industry in the rainforest. If developed countries won't set an example, why should developing countries save their rainforests?

Why does burning the forest down add to the problem of global warming?

What can we do?

The Earth Summit produced an important agreement about biodiversity. It talks about preserving the variety of life on this planet. Agenda 21 says we should try to replant trees wherever we can.

What can you do? Ask DIY stores where they get their hardwoods. Some have already agreed not to trade in mahogany.

Think about where the beef for your kingsize burgers comes from.

Endangered species

Every day, it is estimated that fifty species of plants and animals are lost from this planet. Many others are coming close to extinction. We call these the endangered species and they include some of the big mammals such as the black rhinoceros and the mountain gorilla. A report from the United Nations says that 25 per cent of all species could be extinct by the middle of the 21st century.

Human survival depends on the existence and survival of millions of other species. Through our thoughtless actions, we are endangering other species and steadily reducing the biodiversity on this planet.

Becoming extinct

These animals (below) are in danger of becoming extinct (dying out) as they lose their habitats and are hunted for their horns or skins.

The Arabian oryx actually became extinct in the wild in 1972. Some zoos have managed to breed this animal in captivity and have since reintroduced it into the wild.

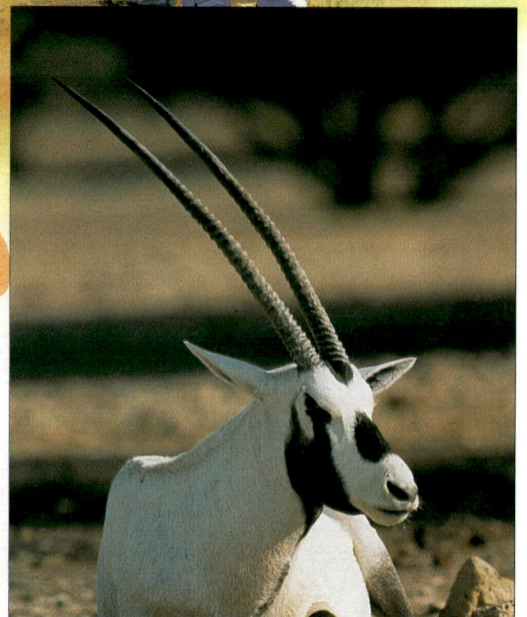

Trading in endangered species

Birds The photo shows the Spix-macaw, a species like a parrot from the Amazon rainforest in Brazil. This bird is rapidly disappearing from the rainforests. It is sold illegally for up to £5000.

Bears Five of the eight species of bear are in danger. Some people believe that eating certain parts of the bear can help prevent them getting heart or liver disease.

Rhinoceros/elephants The rhinoceros horn is thought to have special medicinal powers by some people in Asia. Poachers make a living by killing animals and selling their tusks and horns. Other people make ornaments and jewellery from the ivory.

Why do you think the Spix-macaw is rapidly disappearing from the rainforests?

As the human population grows people clear the forest, build homes and plant crops. Many endangered plants and animals are being squeezed into smaller and smaller areas where their habitat is still untouched.

Poachers' ivory being burned in Nairobi

What can we do?

Agenda 21 says we should protect the biodiversity of this planet. But we shoot animals for their skins, furs, horns and tusks, we force them out of their natural habitats and we pollute their environment.

CITES is the Convention on International Trade in Endangered Species which regulates the world-wide trade in threatened animals and plants. This is action taking at a global level.

What can you do? You could join an organisation such as WWF-UK, which helps conserve animals, plants and habitats for the benefit of all life on Earth.

Deserting the Earth

During the 1980s, about 3 million people around the world died through poverty and starvation. Many of these people were trying to live from a land where the soil was too poor to support their crops or cattle. Through over-grazing, less rainfall and deforestation, the land had been turned into a kind of desert. This is called desertification. Today, it is estimated that a quarter of the surface of the Earth is at risk from desertification.

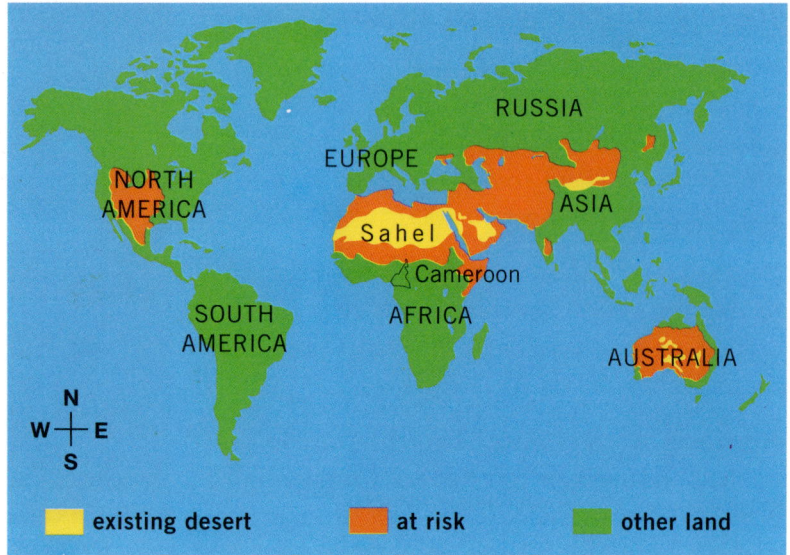

More than a billion people are affected by desertification. Which countries are most affected, and where are they?

Damaging the land

Look at the two photos below. They show how we can spoil the environment.

In the first photo, the land is well covered in vegetation. It can sustain (provide food for) the local nomadic people who roam from place to place. As long as they don't stay too long before finding fresh grazing for their cattle, the land will have time to recover before they come back again.

The second photo shows a very damaged environment. The vegetation is gone and

This land can sustain nomadic people and their cattle.

Cutting down trees and overgrazing the vegetation has exposed the soil to erosion.

the land can't sustain the people any more. In order to survive, the people have had no choice but to cut down the trees for firewood and to let their cattle over-graze the vegetation.

Good land becomes poor land when it is over-grazed and deforested and there is little rainfall. The soil has lost its fertility and cannot support plant life. Any water soon evaporates and the soil becomes dry and loose. The wind then blows it away. This is called erosion.

Harvesting cotton in Vina Valley, Cameroon. Cotton is a 'cash crop'.

Why is this happening?

Why do nomadic people over-graze their land? They usually have no choice. It is often the government which decides how their land is used. If some of their land is taken and used for other purposes, they don't have so much space. So they have to return too quickly to graze the land they have only recently left. In order to live sustainably, they must have the freedom to roam widely across the land.

Cash crops

Have you ever thought about where your packet of peanuts comes from? They could have come from the Sahel. Look at the map on page 20 to see where that is.

Peanuts are often grown on land in the Sahel which used to be traditional nomadic grazing land. They are grown to earn money. This is why they are called 'cash crops'.

Think about what this means for the nomads. How much land will be left for them?

What can we do?

Agenda 21 points out that poverty, starvation and desertification are all closely linked. What do you think about the rights and wrongs of the solutions suggested below?

■ Cash crops should be banned from areas at risk from desertification.

■ Nomadic people should be prevented from roaming the land and over-grazing it.

■ Local people should be given regular food aid from abroad.

What can you do? You could ask about which other products are grown for cash and where they come from. Some suggestions are tea, coffee, chocolate or soya.

Mountains of waste

The United Kingdom produces about 20 million tonnes of household rubbish every year. Most of it is buried in holes in the ground. But the UK is a small country and most people are not keen on living in an environment with so much buried rubbish. Burning the rubbish is possible, but that too has problems. Why do we produce so much waste in the first place?

Filling holes in the ground

The cheapest way of getting rid of rubbish is to fill up holes in the ground (landfill sites). But there are problems. Toxins (poisons) from the rubbish can seep into the earth and pollute the ground water. Organic rubbish, such as food and garden waste, rots. It is a health hazard and it produces a gas called methane which can cause explosions.

For this reason, most rubbish tips are not suitable for building on. Housing developments have been built on some reclaimed tips, but there have been problems. Great care has to be taken to ensure that the site is decontaminated and that the methane gas can escape through specially built vents.

This is a landfill site in Cheshire. Can you think why it is getting harder to find landfill sites?

Should rubbish be burnt?

About 9 per cent of our household rubbish is incinerated (burnt), but this is expensive, even if the heat is used to make electricity. Burning it also produces greenhouse gases and can release toxins, such as dioxin, into the atmosphere.

What's in the rubbish?

Look at the picture. If you sorted and weighed your rubbish, you could see if it is similar to this.

It's been discovered recently that people are discouraged from sorting different materials for recycling if they only have to put all their rubbish in a large wheelie bin.

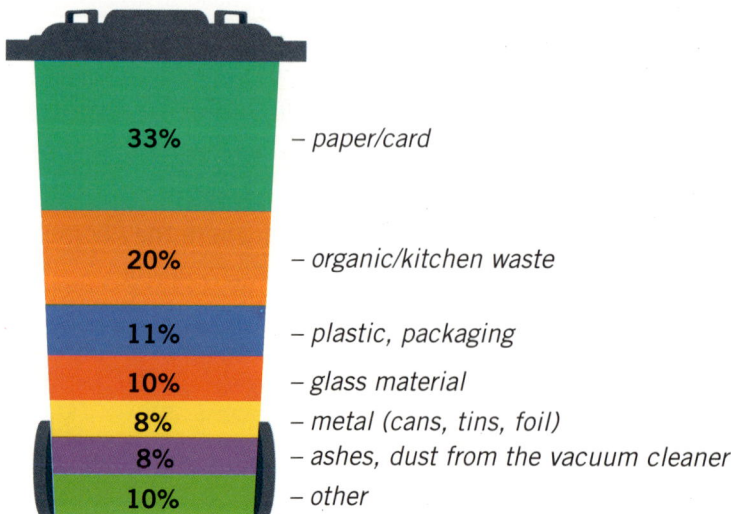

33%	– paper/card
20%	– organic/kitchen waste
11%	– plastic, packaging
10%	– glass material
8%	– metal (cans, tins, foil)
8%	– ashes, dust from the vacuum cleaner
10%	– other

What a waste!

Look at the photos and ask yourself this question. Is it really necessary to produce so much waste?

How long do we use plastic packaging before it is thrown away?

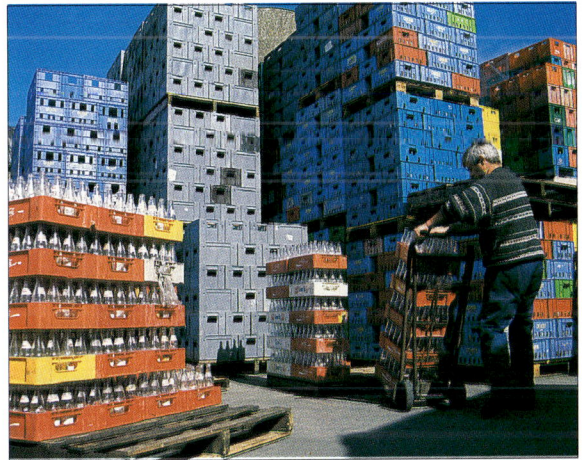

What other sort of container can we get milk in?

Why don't we buy all our drinks in returnable bottles?

What can we do?

Twenty million tonnes of rubbish is a massive amount of rubbish to throw away every year. Some local councils now provide kerbside collection services for collecting domestic waste for recycling. It seems that if recycling is made easy, most people are willing to co-operate.

What can you do? Find out what recycling services are available in your area. Contact the local council and Friends of the Earth.

The three Rs for the environment

Radioactive waste

Some radioactive waste comes from industry and hospitals but most comes from nuclear power stations. It is a serious environmental problem – all we can do is store it. But where? At sea? Deep underground? If it leaks out, will it harm us, or will it harm future generations? Some people tell us that it is safe, but others say there is no such thing as a safe level of radioactivity.

Is radioactivity natural?

Yes it is. It is called background radiation and there are natural 'hotspots' in some areas of the United Kingdom. Radon gas escapes naturally from granite rocks in the south west of England and the Grampian area of Scotland.

GRAMPIAN
● Aberdeen

N
W — E
S

DEVON
CORNWALL

█ background radiation

Background radiation occurs naturally in some places in the United Kingdom.

Chernobyl power station, USSR, 1986. The nuclear reactor melted down and then exploded. The radiation affected the quality of this photo!

Is radioactive waste safe?

The environmental disaster at Chernobyl on 26 April 1986 has not helped people accept nuclear power as a safe way to generate electricity.

A large area around Chernobyl was soon heavily contaminated by radioactive fallout. Material from the explosion was also carried up into the atmosphere and drifted across Europe.

Fallout from Chernobyl contaminated land all across the north of the British Isles. Ten years later, some sheep farmers have only just been allowed to sell their lamb again.

Most people are afraid of radioactive waste because its effects last for years.

There are three types of radioactive waste that come from nuclear power stations. These are low level, intermediate level and high level. At the moment, all intermediate and high level radioactive wastes have to be held in stores which are run by the government.

Nuclear power

Countries with limited reserves of fossil fuels (see page 86), such as Japan and France, generate most of their electricity at nuclear power stations. They say nuclear power has environmental advantages.

- It does not release greenhouse gases.

- It does not create acid rain.

- One tonne of nuclear fuel produces as much electricity as 150 000 tonnes of coal.

Nuclear power

These are the kinds of questions that people ask:

- What are we going to do with the intermediate and high level waste?

- What are the chances of there being another Chernobyl?

- For how long will the power station still be radioactive when it comes to the end of its life?

- What should we do with the plutonium that comes from reprocessing fuel rods? (Plutonium can be used for making nuclear weapons.)

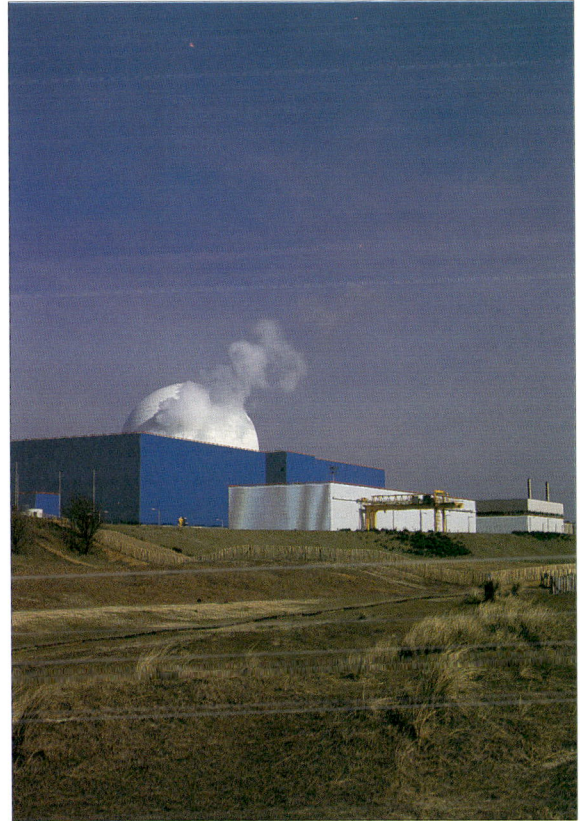

Sizewell B is the latest nuclear power station to be built in the UK, and it could be the last.

What can we do?

France cut its release of greenhouse gases by 80 per cent in seven years by generating electricity from nuclear power. This is good news for global warming. But having read about the advantages and disadvantages of nuclear power, do you think this is the way to generate electricity in the future?

What can you do? Find out more about the arguments for and against nuclear power. Try contacting Nuclear Electric (British Fuel), or organisations such as Friends of the Earth or Greenpeace.

Reduce, reuse, recycle

The developed world has become known as a 'throwaway society' which depends on using up materials extracted from the environment and then throwing them away. Cheap plastics, for instance, have made this possible. The developing world, however, has millions of people who try to reuse, repair and recycle materials wherever possible. At the moment, they produce a lot less waste than we do.

These shoes in a Kenyan market have been made from old car tyres.

Can the developed world continue with this 'throwaway' approach? What if the developing world tries to do the same? Resources won't last forever. How long will the supply of oil last if everyone uses it at the rate of the developed world?

The three Rs

Look at the pictures. Think of other ways you could reduce, reuse and recycle.

What is recycled?

The materials most often recycled are glass, paper and metal. Plastics are the hardest to recycle because there are so many different types which can't be mixed and melted down like glass or metal.

Paper

Three million tonnes of paper are recycled each year.

Glass

Half a million tonnes of glass are recycled every year.

Metal

Recycled metal is a profitable business. Aluminium can fetch £600 per tonne.

Plastic

It's estimated that, by the year 2000, more than a billion tonnes of plastic around the world will be thrown away each year.

Clothes

Old clothes can be taken to charities such as Age Concern and Oxfam.

Biodegradable plastics

We can now make plastics which eventually break down when exposed to light for a certain length of time. There are advantages and disadvantages to this. Does it solve any of the problems? Is it a sustainable way of using materials from the environment (see page 54)?

Is recycling always best?

In Thailand, recycling paper has caused problems. It's not the paper that's the problem, but the ink that is removed during recycling – it pollutes the rivers.

Plastic is difficult to recycle but it can be used to make things like T-shirts!

What can you do?

Local Agenda 21

All councils must publish a strategy (plan) for recycling. Ring up or write to your local council to find out how you could get involved (see page 52).

Eco Schools

Contact Going for Green to find out more about the Eco Schools Project.

Action Earth

You could join a national project such as Action Earth which could help you meet other people who care about the environment. Ring Community Service Volunteers (CSV Environment).

Fresh water

Providing fresh water for everyone in the 21st Century is not going to be easy. At the moment, a third of the countries around the world don't get enough – even for their basic needs. In the developed countries, things are very different. People expect to get pure, high quality water through their taps whenever they wish. Although the Earth is covered in water, less than 1 per cent is actually fresh. The rest is salt water.

Water in the developing countries

The map (below) shows the countries around the world where fresh water is not so safe to drink. Look at other maps in this book to see where deforestation and desertification are happening (see pages 64 and 68). What do you notice?

Global change

We know that industry and the use of the car could be changing the atmospheric environment and affecting weather patterns around the globe. Could global

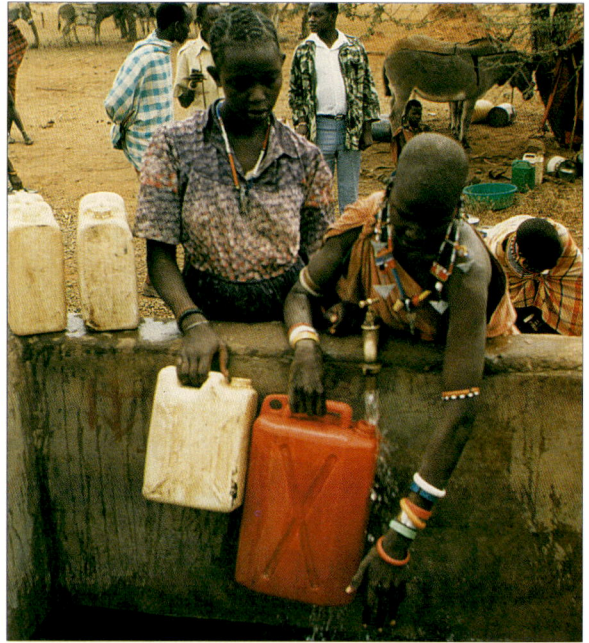

In Kenya, the systems for collecting and piping water to the people are very poor. In rural areas, most people have to fetch and carry it.

warming be damaging countries which are short of fresh water?

If the Earth warms even by a degree or two, it could upset the pattern of rainfall around the world. Some countries might get more rain and others might get less.

Local change

Could cutting down forests be changing local climates and weather patterns? Rainforests soak up rain like a sponge. Water moves back and forth between the forests and the air. If you cut down the trees, the local climate will almost certainly change. It could also lead to soil erosion and desertification (see page 68).

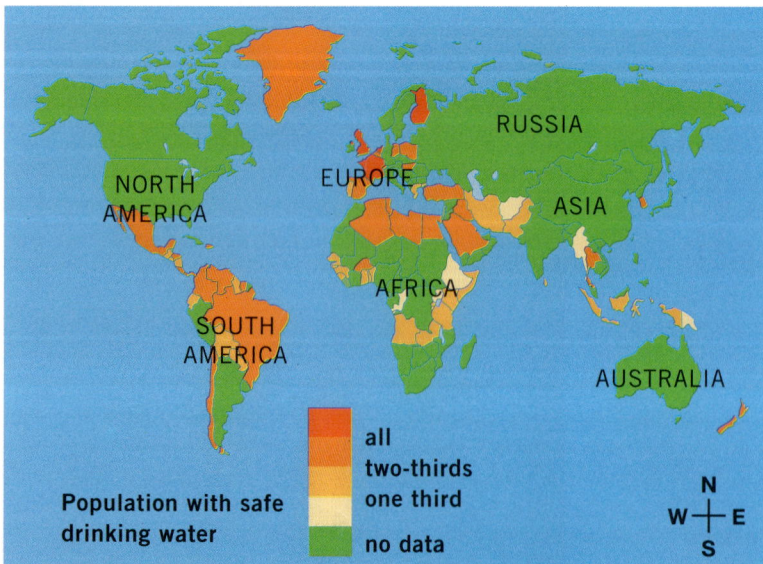

Population with safe drinking water: all / two-thirds / one third / no data

Where are most of the countries where water is not so safe to drink?

Water in the developed countries

People in the developed countries expect pure water to be on tap. The European Union sets standards on quality so that our water is almost 100 per cent pure. It must also be free of microbes. That's why it often smells of chlorine. The demand for more and more water is steadily increasing. Why? The pictures (below) might give you a clue.

It's thought that each person in the developed world uses about 150 litres of water every day, but uses only 3 litres for drinking and cooking. The rest is 'wasted'.

Somehow, we are still not satisfied with our tap water and many of us are now buying bottled water for drinking. Unfortunately, this water comes in plastic containers which immediately creates another environmental problem. Why do you think people buy bottled water?

What can we do?

At the moment, 25 per cent of people on this Earth don't get safe drinking water. Agenda 21 recommends that, by the year 2025, there should be safe water for everyone to use. It's not really possible to transport water around the world, and it's too expensive to take the salt out of seawater (desalination). The most helpful thing we can all do is try to reduce our release of greenhouse gases into the atmosphere.

What can you do? Look at the pictures on this page. Think about how much water is 'wasted'. Perhaps you could change the way you use water.

These pictures show how water is 'wasted'.

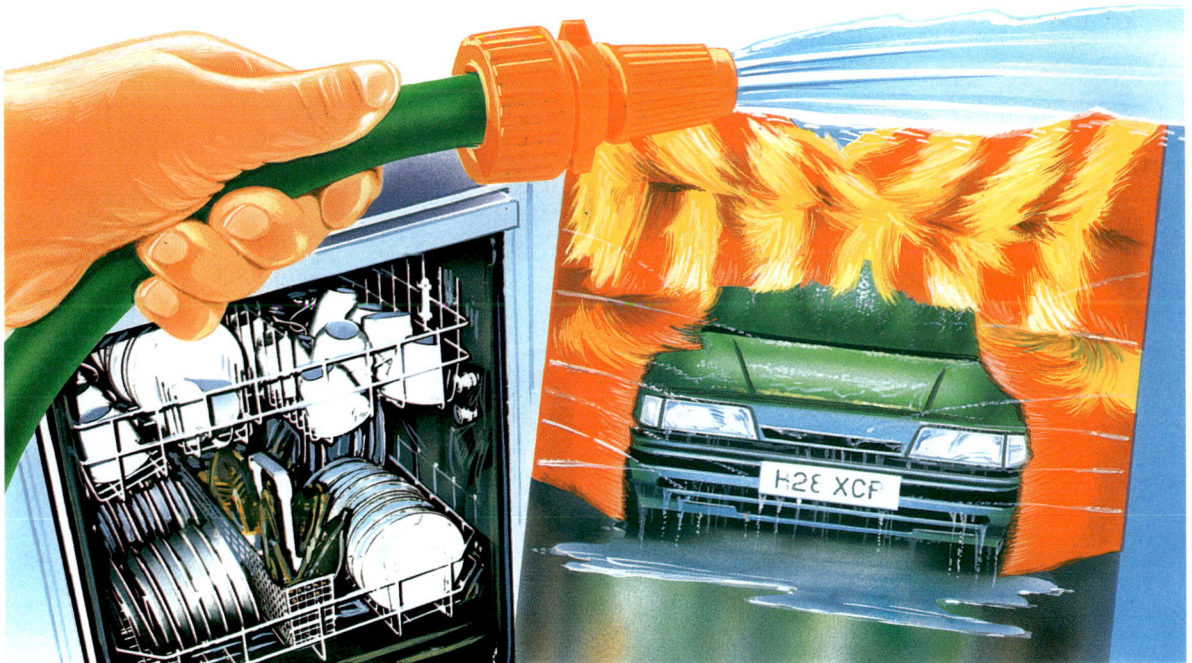

Seaworld

The seas around the British Isles are a cheap dumping ground for chemical waste. We dump sewage, chemicals, oil and radioactive waste. But what are we doing to the environment of millions of plant and animal species that live in this underwater world? Do we know what chemicals could be coming back to us through the food chain when we eat animals and plants from the sea?

20% of toxic waste in the North Sea flows from British rivers.

Where is all the waste coming from?

Two million tonnes of toxic (poisonous) waste flow out of the major rivers into the seas around the British Isles. Toxic waste includes fertilisers, pesticides, radioactive material and heavy metals (e.g. lead, mercury). Some of this waste comes from chemical and other industries, but fertilisers and pesticides simply run off farmers' land into the rivers. All these pollutants can get into the food chain, but the most worrying are the fertilisers and pesticides that enter the sea in such large quantities.

Look at the map (above). Why do you think the river Rhine carries more waste than all the others? Notice where it starts.

Some beaches have been awarded the blue flag. This means the water is safe for bathing. What might be wrong with the beaches that are not awarded a blue flag?

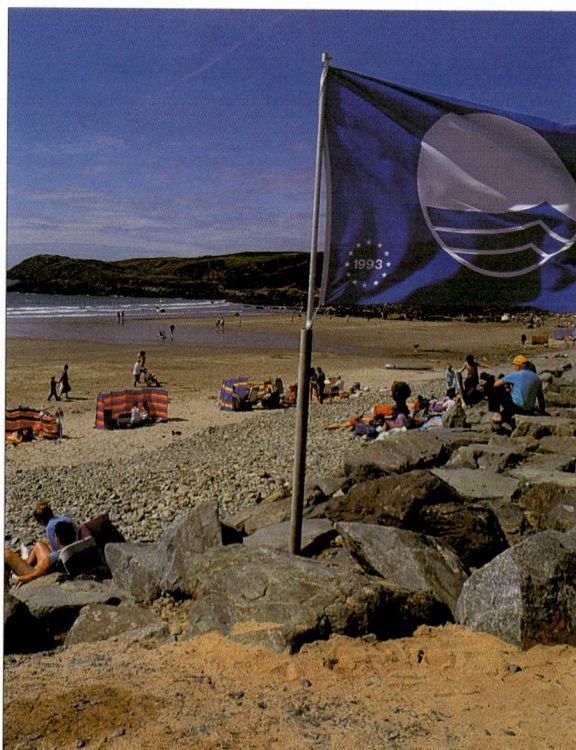

This beach in Dyfed, Wales has been awarded the blue flag for being clean and safe.

If the sea becomes cloudy, what might happen to the food chain? Why?

Are we damaging the sea?

People argue that because the sea is so enormous, any waste we tip into it is soon diluted and broken down. Look at the picture above. It shows how sewage sludge could disturb food chains in the sea.

What can we do?

Agenda 21 says we should protect our coastlines from pollution. But this isn't easy. It is already against the law to dump oil at sea, but more oil still comes from ships cleaning their tanks illegally than comes from disasters such as the *Exxon Valdez* or the *Sea Empress* (1996). All we can do is try to reduce our need for oil.

Sewage sludge dumping in the North Sea

Tourism

Have you ever been on a package holiday abroad? It was probably to a place with different people to you and with a different way of life. Package holidays have opened up the world to global travel. This has brought benefits to many poorer countries by bringing in valuable cash, but it has also had a serious effect on their environments. What effect might you be having on other parts of the world when you travel? Are you environmentally responsible?

What's the problem?

By the year 2000, the number of tourists travelling abroad each year will reach 700 million. Tourists want to travel to more and more exotic places which then struggle to cope with the needs of so many extra people. Think about the problems being shown in these photos.

Clearing trees to make ski slopes in the French Alps has created an earthslip.

Vehicle pollution can damage the plant and animal life. The noise can also cause distress to some animals, like the cheetah, who leave their kills uneaten.

Eco tourism

Eco tourism is about trying to keep the balance between the needs of the tourist and the ability of the local environment to cope. If there isn't a balance, then the result will be environmental damage.

Green travel

Some tour operators offer 'green' package holidays which are sensitive to the environment being visited. These tour operators are likely to be members of CERT (Campaign for Environmentally Responsible Tourism). Look for the logo:

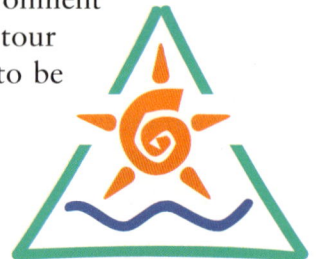

Campaign for Environmentally Responsible Tourism

It is also possible to join special environmental research expeditions such as Earthwatch or the British Schools Exploring Society. (You must be over 16.)

Earthwatch is an international science foundation which works to sustain the world's environment, monitor global change and conserve endangered species.

The British Schools Exploring Society involves young people working in remote corners of the world on a range of projects that contribute to our understanding of the environment.

What can you do?

There are some simple things you can do when you travel abroad on holiday:

■ Be environmentally sensitive – other countries are not necessarily like yours. Each country has its own environment with different people and a different way of life which should be respected.

■ Don't buy products made from endangered species (see page 66).

■ Don't leave litter – if it's plastic, take it back home.

■ Reduce the amount of water you use – water is scarce and valuable.

Carnival time, Rio de Janeiro. Every country has its own environment and culture which should be respected.

Transport

In the developed world, the car is a way of life. It is seen as essential for work and for leisure. People enjoy the freedom to get around as and when they like. However, there are environmental costs to be paid. As well as using up non-renewable fuel, cars produce greenhouse gases and poisonous fumes that pollute the air we breathe.

Global effects

Every time you use the car you are adding carbon dioxide to the atmosphere, and contributing to global warming. In the developed world, about 25 per cent of the carbon dioxide comes from traffic. The freedom of the open road is the dream of most motorists, and some people may be lucky enough to find one.

Lots of people experience traffic like this.

A traffic jam in Bangkok. Is this how the future will look?

It's thought, for example, that an average German motorist spends 65 hours a year stuck in traffic jams, and this will double over the next twenty years. But it's not just a problem in the developed world. We are now finding just the same problems in the big cities of the developing world.

Taking your breath away

Although petrol and diesel cars both produce carbon dioxide and other pollutants, it is not clear which of them causes the most pollution.

Breathing in car fumes is hazardous to health. If the cyclist has breathing problems like asthma or bronchitis, then car fumes will make these problems worse. The fumes can also cause other problems such as heart disease and cancer.

Smog in Mexico City

Smog

Chemical reactions involving car fumes are sparked off by bright sunlight and make ozone. At ground level, ozone is extremely poisonous. Where is ozone an important gas?

Are there any solutions?

Some countries in the developed world now have strict standards about pollutants from car exhaust pipes. Some insist that catalytic converters are fitted (see below).

Catalytic converters can only be fitted to cars that run on unleaded fuel, and they only work efficiently when they are fully warmed up. As most journeys are between three and five miles, is the catalytic converter a real solution?

Carving a way forward!

Cars need roads, and roads need space. A new bypass, therefore, makes great changes to people's local environments. Do you agree or disagree with the following statements:

■ New roads cause motorists to make more journeys.

■ Bypasses improve the health of people living in the town.

■ Habitats for wildlife are more important than roads.

■ Bypasses reduce traffic jams.

■ People living in the path of the new road lose their homes, but the local community will benefit.

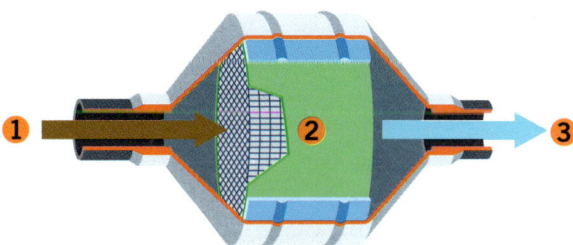

1 exhaust fumes enter here

2 nitrogen and sulphur oxides, hydrocarbons and particulates are removed

3 pollutants are reduced but carbon dioxide is still present

What can we do?

Today, there are 500 million cars worldwide. The motor industry is developing 'lean burn' engines which will use less fuel. But if we drive more miles, we are still pumping greenhouse gases into the air. The easiest solution is for governments to make driving very expensive.

What can you do? Find out what your family and friends think about their cars. Would they give them up or use them less?

Transport tomorrow

Are cars a danger to health, and a threat to the environment through the global warming they cause? How many jobs are involved in building cars and trucks and using them to transport goods? Will people ever give up the personal freedom they get from a car which allows them to go where and when they like? Your answers to these questions could shape the future of your environment.

Tram system, Manchester. Investing in public transport is expensive. Does it encourage drivers to leave their cars at home?

Looking for alternatives

Each of the pictures on this page represents an idea which could reduce carbon dioxide emissions as well as reducing health risks from pollution. What does each picture suggest to you? What are the problems with each idea?

A Park and Ride terminus in Cambridge. People still use their cars to get to the terminus!

If cycling was safer, would you prefer to make your journeys on a bike?

An electric car. Where does electricity that is used to charge the batteries come from?

Private or public transport?

All sorts of vehicles are made from non-renewable resources. These vehicles also use up non-renewable fuels to make them go. They release greenhouse gases which add to global warming, and poisonous gases which damage people's health. They can also cause dreadful congestion.

More cars mean more roads. New roads can destroy people's homes and rare wildlife habitats. They can also encourage people to drive even more. Vehicles can also kill thousands of people every year. With so many disadvantages, why are people so reluctant to give up or reduce the use of their cars?

If you ask motorists why they won't use public transport, they often say:

■ There aren't any buses or trains available.

■ It's much more expensive.

■ It doesn't go where you want to go.

■ You have to wait, so it takes longer.

■ You have to share and it's not so comfortable.

■ You can't carry lots of things.

■ The motor industry creates jobs for people.

What can we do?

How could we make public transport more attractive to people in the future? Here are some suggestions for you to think about:

■ Build lots of new public transport systems.

■ Make it cheap to travel on public transport.

■ Make car drivers pay road tolls to drive in urban areas.

■ Introduce traffic calming systems to slow traffic right down.

■ Only allow electric cars in urban areas.

■ Make all city centres for pedestrians and cyclists only.

■ Ban private transport from city centres when pollution levels are high.

What can you do? Imagine you are a car driver and still want to use your car, but you feel strongly that you must try to reduce the damage your car has on the environment. These pictures (below) will give you some ideas of what you could do.

Coal, gas and oil

Do you burn coal, gas or oil (fossil fuels) in your home, or use products that are made from them? Most people in industrial countries do. They rely on coal, gas and oil for making electricity, and for producing consumer goods.

Unfortunately, all the processes needed to get coal, gas and oil out of the ground, and the uses we have for them, cause damage to the environment in one way or another. What would be a more sustainable way of using these fossil fuels without damaging the environment?

Look at the pictures and think about the sort of environmental damage that might be happening in each case.

Transporting oil

There are major oil fields around the world. The problem is that once the oil has been extracted from the ground or

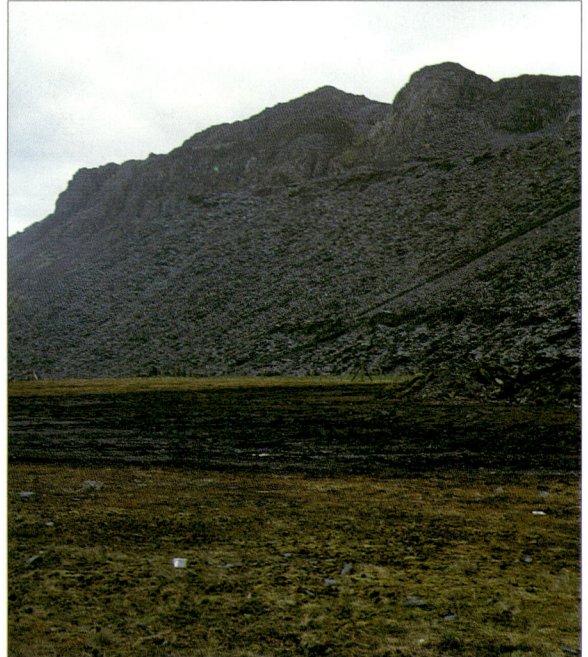

Spoil from a slate mine, Wales. If it rains heavily, what will happen?

sea, it has to be transported to oil refineries. This can be done over land by huge pipelines or by sea in massive tankers which carry 120 000 tonnes of oil at a time.

The *Sea Empress* lost over 65 000 tonnes of oil into the UK's Maritime Nature Reserve before it was eventually floated off the rocks.

Oil is not the only cause of environmental damage. Detergent is sprayed on the oil slick to break it up and stop it washing on to the beaches. This spray produces even more toxic chemicals which damage the vital food chains in the sea.

The ocean wastebin

The Brent Spar is the remains of a massive North Sea oil rig. It contains toxic metals, such as lead and mercury, and also hydrocarbons, organic compounds and radioactive drilling fluids.

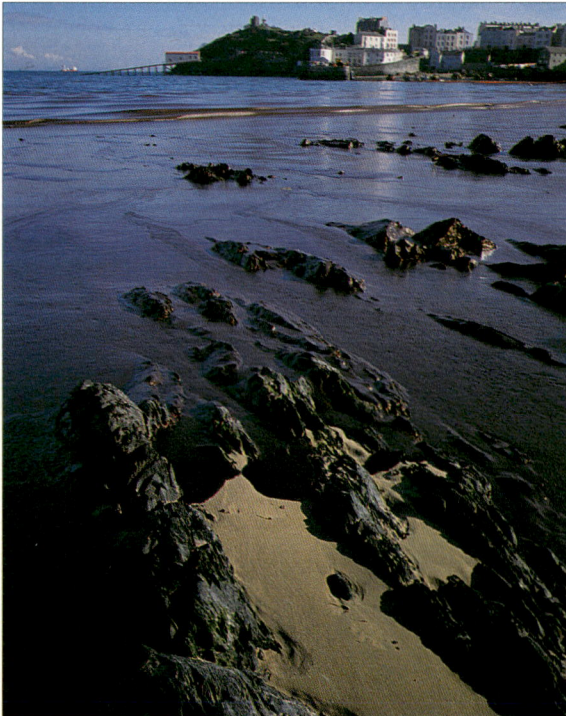

Oil lost from the Sea Empress, *Tenby, Wales*

The Shell Oil Company wanted to dump the Brent Spar in 2000 metres of water, far out in the Atlantic Ocean. It's thought that it takes water from this depth at least 250 years before it returns to the surface. By this time, all the poisons should be broken up. Greenpeace were against dumping the rig. They argued that it should be decontaminated and recycled instead. There are many more rigs still out in the North Sea. How do you think they should be disposed of?

The Brent Spar is towed from the Atlantic into a Norwegian fjord.

Fossil fuel power stations

Burning coal, gas or oil to make electricity produces pollutants such as carbon dioxide, sulphur dioxide and nitrogen oxides. Look at this table:

Power station	CO_2	SO_2	NO_x
Coal	✔	✔	✔
Oil	✔	✔	✘
Gas	✔	✘	✘

Why will all three contribute to global warming? Which types of power stations are likely to produce acid rain?

Consumer goods

Coal and oil are rich raw materials which can be used to manufacture consumer goods such as plastic cups and textiles. Think about the following questions:

■ Why do we burn fossil fuels if they cause global warming?

■ Why do we use them to make throwaway goods?

■ Why are these goods so difficult to get rid of?

■ Why do we burn them if we can make things from them?

■ What will we use when the coal, gas and oil have run out (see pages 88–9)?

What can we do?
We all know that fossil fuels will run out soon, but it doesn't stop us using our cars, central heating, air conditioning or electrical goods. How can we change the attitudes and behaviour of people in the developed countries?

What can you do? Get in contact with your Local Agenda 21 group and find out what you can do to help.

Alternative energy

The developed countries make most of their electricity from fossil fuels and nuclear power. But fossil fuels produce greenhouse gases and acid rain, and nuclear power produces radioactive waste. All of these damage the environment. The search is on, therefore, for other ways of making electricity which do less damage to the environment.

Environment friendly

Are all alternative ways of making electricity friendly to the environment? Ask yourself these questions to decide what the advantages and disadvantages of an alternative are:

- Will it add to global warming?

- How much electricity will it generate?

- How much energy will it take to build it and how expensive will it be to run?

- What effect will it have on the local environment?

– Will people have to move?

– Will wildlife habitats be destroyed?

– Will it be a blot on the landscape?

- How long will it last and what will happen to it at the end of its life?

- Will it produce waste disposal problems?

Use these questions to help you think about the environmental impact of these alternative ways of making electricity. You won't know all the answers but you will get an idea of the problems. Look at the examples on these pages:

Solar cells collect sunlight and use the energy to make electricity.

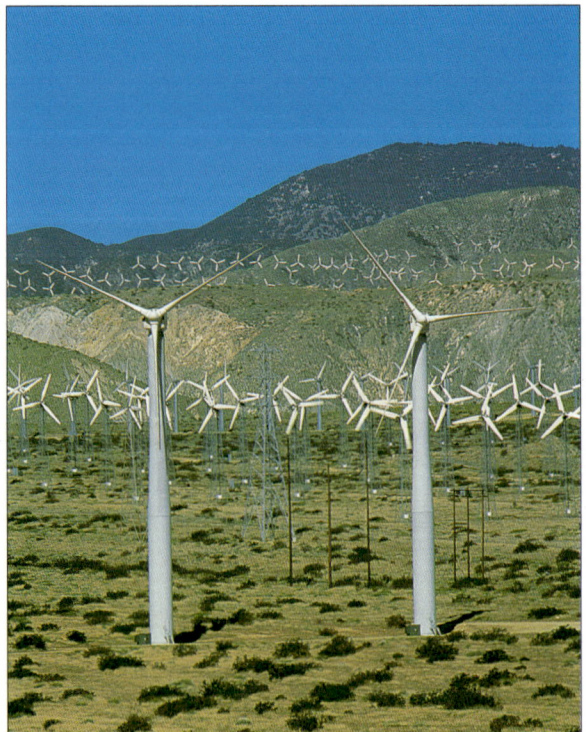

Wind turbines produce no emissions and have a low running cost.

A hydro-electric power station in Sri Lanka

A tidal barrage. The movement energy in the tides can be used to make electricity, but a massive barrier has to be built to do it.

Hydro-electric power station

A dam holding back billions of litres of water is a massive store of energy which can be used to make electricity. But a dam creates a reservoir, which floods the land behind it and affects the waterflow downstream.

Local people feel strongly about these schemes. Can you think why? Hydro-electric power stations are very expensive. They also cause many environmental changes both during the building process and afterwards. But they don't produce greenhouse gases.

Biomass fuels

Many native people in developing countries get their fuel from wood, charcoal and animal dung. Think about the environmental advantages and disadvantages of using these energy sources.

What can we do?

Electricity is vital in developed countries as high standards of living depend on it. The developing countries also see this as the way to improve their standard of living.

What do you think of the future of fossil fuels and nuclear power for generating electricity? Do you think we should be looking for new sustainable sources of energy?

What can you do? Ring your Local Agenda 21 group for some ideas.

Action taking

Action taking is about your contribution to caring for this planet. For many of you it will be about choosing 'green' (environmentally friendly) products and becoming informed. Action taking depends on how you see the planet being preserved in the future, and how we can provide for the needs of future generations.

Think globally, act locally

You may feel that there is not much you can do on your own about the big issues concerning the environment. Acting locally means that lots of people acting together can make a real difference on a global scale. Through your actions, you can inform others and encourage 'green' actions by lots of other people. Turn to pages 52 and 53 for ideas of how you can get involved locally.

You could hold a recycling sale with friends.

Environmental audit

The point of an environmental audit is to help you to find out how wasteful or efficient you are in the use of resources. You can then take action to reduce the amount of energy, water and other resources which you use and find ways to reduce the level of waste. These actions may not only make you 'greener', but they may save you money as well.

Water

Make a list of all the ways you use water. Here are some ideas:

Water	litres per day
■ making tea/coffee	
■ taking a bath	
■ washing up	
■ flushing the toilet	

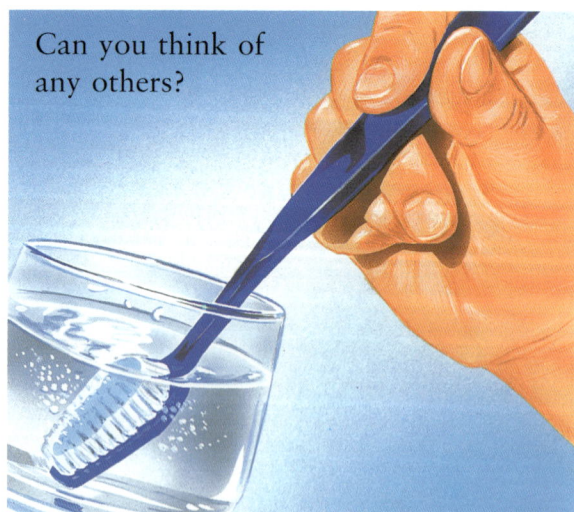

Can you think of any others?

Household rubbish

The average household produces 10–15 kg of rubbish per week. It's estimated that 70 per cent of all household rubbish can be recycled. How close can you get to this?

Collect one day's rubbish. Separate and weigh the different types of rubbish. Draw a pie graph or chart to show what's in your waste. Decide what percentage of waste you could recycle if you really wanted to.

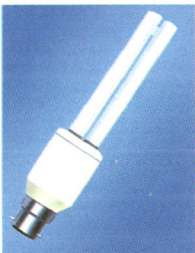

Energy

The way you use electricity and fuel in the home has a direct effect on the environment. The more you use, the more greenhouse gases are released either from your home or at the power station.

Check out your home. Do you have:

	Yes	No
■ draught proofed doors/windows		
■ low energy light bulbs fitted		
■ hot water pipes/tank lagged		
■ thermostatic valves on radiators		
■ loft insulation		
■ plastic double glazing fitted		
■ cavity wall insulation		

As a result of taking action, every unit of electricity (kilowatt hour) you save from your electricity bill can save the power station releasing 1 kg of carbon dioxide.

Travel

How many miles does the family car do each week?

Check out your travel. Make a checklist of journeys and number of miles each day for a week. Here are some ideas:

Journey	Miles
■ trip to school and back	
■ trip to supermarket	
■ trip to football game	

For each journey, think about whether it could be done using another form of transport, such as walking, bicycle, bus, train, or sharing a lift. Decide when you prefer to use the car.

Each litre of petrol releases about 2 kg of carbon dioxide into the atmosphere. Find out how many miles per gallon your car does. (1 gallon = 4.5 litres)

Try making some journeys without the car. Work out how many kilos of carbon are saved from going into the atmosphere.

Glossary

acid rain   Rain containing acid that comes from gases in the air such as sulphur dioxide

biodiversity   The wide range of species of plants, animals and microbes living on this planet. The word comes from *bio* meaning 'life' and *diversity* meaning 'varied'.

CFC   Short for chloro-fluoro-carbon. It is a man-made gas which breaks up the ozone layer. It is an ODS (see page 93).

climate   The pattern of weather that occurs in a particular part of the world (e.g. rainforests have a tropical climate)

contaminated   Polluted or poisoned

decontaminated   Free from pollution or poisons

deforestation   The clearing of trees and shrubs from the land

desalination   The process that makes fresh water from sea water

desertification   The process by which soil loses its fertility so that it can no longer support the growth of plants

developed countries   The rich and industrialised countries. People in these countries use up high levels of energy and resources.

developing countries   These are not industrialised and are much poorer than the developed countries. They use far lower levels of energy and resources.

ecosystem   The environment in which plants, animals and microbes are linked together by food chains (e.g. a rainforest or the ocean)

emission   The release of gases which pollute the atmosphere

erosion   The wearing away of soil or rock by wind and water

food chain   Who eats what (e.g. we eat animals which have eaten plants)

fossil fuels   Formed along with fossils many millions of years ago (e.g. coal, gas and oil)

global warming   The steady but slight increase in the temperature of the Earth's atmosphere (also known as the 'greenhouse effect')

greenhouse gases   Gases, such as carbon dioxide, that trap the Sun's energy on the surface of the Earth. They are thought to be the cause of global warming.

habitat   Where a group of plants and animals live (e.g. a hedgerow)

hydro-electric power (HEP)   This comes from water falling from a high level (e.g. top of a dam) to a lower level. The energy from falling water is used to drive turbines which then generate electricity.

industrial countries   Rich countries with highly developed technologies which give most of the people a high standard of living

melanoma   Cancer of the skin

nitrogen oxides (NO$_x$)   Gases emitted from vehicles and industry which pollute the atmosphere

non-renewable resources   These cannot be replaced once they have been used up (e.g. fossil fuels, metals and plastics)

nuclear power   The generation of electricity by the splitting of uranium atoms

ozone depleting substances (ODSs) These break up the ozone layer (e.g. CFCs and freon)

ozone layer   The delicate layer high in the stratosphere that blocks out harmful radiation from the Sun

pesticides   Chemicals designed to kill insects and other animals which would otherwise destroy crops

photochemical smog   Occurs in towns and cities and is caused by sunlight reacting with vehicle pollution

photosynthesise   When plants make their own food from carbon dioxide and water, using light from the Sun

pollution   The poisoning of air, water or land

radioactivity   Released by radioactive materials as they break down. It can be very harmful.

recycling   Making new things out of materials that would otherwise be thrown away

renewable resources   Can be replaced in a fairly short space of time (e.g. paper or wool)

solar cell   Can use the energy from sunlight to generate electricity

solar radiation   The energy that comes from the Sun

stratosphere   The upper part of the atmosphere where the air is very thin and where the ozone layer can be found

sulphur dioxide (SO$_2$)   A pollutant gas that is released mainly from coal-fired power stations. It is the main cause of acid rain.

sustainable development   Meeting the needs of people today without damaging the environment for people in the future

tidal barrage   A barrier built across an estuary which uses the energy in the tides to generate electricity

toxin   A poisonous material

United Nations (UN)   The organisation that brings together most of the countries of the world

unsustainable development   A lifestyle that cannot be supported by the Earth's resources

Published by BBC Educational Publishing, a division of BBC Education, BBC White City, 201 Wood Lane, London W12 7TS

First published in this form 1997
© Keith Bishop/BBC Worldwide (through BBC Education) 1996
The moral right of the author has been asserted.

Colour reproduction by Dot Gradations, Essex
Cover Colour origination in England by Tinsley Robor, London

Acknowledgements
Edited by Debbie Reid
Designed by Sarah Peden
Picture research by Emma Segal

Illustrations: © Maltings Partnership 1996 (pages 55, 58, 60, 64, 68, 70, 72, 76, 78, 79 and 83); © Satchel Illustration 1996 (pages 59, 66, 77, 90 and 91); © Cathy Morley 1996 (pages 56-7)

Photos: BBC/Simon Pugh **pp. 54, 56 (left), 62 (left, right, bottom), 71 (top, left), 74 (bottom right, middle);** Keith Bishop **p. 75;** CERT **p. 80 (bottom right);** Bruce Coleman Collection/Frithfoto **p. 65;** Bruce Coleman Collection/Steven Kaufman **p. 66;** Bruce Coleman Collection/Luiz Claudio

Marigo **p. 81 (bottom);** Earthwatch **p. 81 (top);** EPL/John Arnould **p. 57 (bottom);** EPL/Bill Barclay **p. 61 (top);** EPL/Martin Bond **pp. 73, 88 (top);** EPL/Robert Brook **pp. 56 (top), 86 (top);** EPL/Nigel Dickinson **p. 80 (top);** EPL Neil Dyson **p. 84 (middle);** EPL/P. Fryer **p. 79;** EPL/Dylan Garcia **p. 71 (bottom);** EPL/Herbert Girardet **p. 59;** EPL/Charlotte MacPherson **p. 74 (bottom left);** EPL/Michael Marchant **p. 84 (left);** EPL/John Novis **p. 89 (bottom);** EPL/Trevor Perry **p. 53 right;** EPL/Dominic Sansoni **p. 89 (top);** EPL/Richard Smith **p. 63 (main);** Friends of the Earth **p. 56 (bottom);** Going for Green **p. 52 (right);** Greenpeace Communications/Sims **p. 87;** ICCE/Jacolyn Wakeford **p. 90;** Metrolink/Margaret Robinson **p. 84 (top);** NHPA/David Woodfall **pp. 53 (left), 78;** Panos Pictures/Jean-Léo Dugast **p. 82 (bottom);** Panos Pictures/Jasper Young **p. 86 (bottom);** Planet Earth Pictures/Jonathon Scott **p. 67 (bottom left);** Premium/Robert Harding Picture Library **p. 57 (top);** Rex Features **p. 72;** Science Photo Library/Martin Bond **p. 61 (bottom);** Science Photo Library/Simon Fraser **p. 88 (bottom);** Science Photo Library/NASA **p. 50;** Science Photo Library/NOAA **p. 62 (top);** Science Photo Library/David Parker **p. 82 (top);** Science Photo Library/James Stevenson **p. 63 (inset);** Southern Electric **p. 84 (bottom right);** Still Pictures/DRA **p. 51;** Still Pictures/David Drain **p. 70;** Still Pictures/Mark Edwards **pp. 52 (left), 64, 68 (left and right), 69;** Still Pictures/Julio Etchart/Reportage **p. 83;** Still Pictures/Paul Harrison **p. 74 (top);** Still Pictures/John Maier **p. 67 (top);** Still Pictures/Alain Pons **p. 57 (right);** Still Pictures/Jorgen Schytte **p. 76;** WWF-UK **p. 67 (bottom right)**

Wayland Publishers Ltd for the bar chart on page 58

WEATHER

Written by

Tony Potter

Illustrated by

Robin Lawrie

CONTENTS

About this book

Every day there are hundreds of weather forecasts – on TV, radio, in the newspapers and on special weather phone lines. The weather is in the news too, with devastating hurricanes, terrible droughts and even gloomy stories of how the weather is changing. Some say the weather is getting hotter, others that it is getting colder...

This book is a guide to the basics – from why it rains to how hurricanes are formed, with a look at just what might happen in the future. You can find out how the weather affects our lives – and animals' lives too. There are facts and records and explanations of amazing weather tricks. There is even a weather station of your own to make!

A view of Earth's weather from a weather satellite

Weather is the wind, the sunshine, the rain and the snow. It's the cold that numbs your toes and the heat that warms your body. To scientists, weather is the state of the air, or atmosphere, at any particular time or place.

In some places, the weather is much the same day after day. In other places, such as Britain, the weather changes so much that it is difficult to tell what will happen even a few hours ahead. The usual pattern of weather in one place is called its climate.

Weather is an endless cycle of events – from clouds, snow and rain, to lightning, hail and hurricanes. All these are made from three basic ingredients constantly at work like a giant machine in the atmosphere: water, wind and heat from the Sun.

The weather machine is very complicated. Scientists, called meteorologists, study the weather to understand how the machine works. All round the world, 24 hours a day, meteorologists record what is happening to the weather. From this they are able to make forecasts of how the weather is going to change.

Weather words
This book introduces many weather words. You can check what they mean on page 141.

Where does weather happen?
The Earth is surrounded by a thin layer of gases that protect us from extremes of heat or cold. These layers are called the atmosphere. The lowest layer is called the troposphere. This is where all the weather happens.

Satellites

Stratopause

Stratosphere

40km

30km

Ozone layer

The weather only happens up to this height.

20km

Concorde

Tropopause

Airliner

Highest clouds

10km

Troposphere

Mount Everest

Bird

Sea level

Living with the weather

The weather affects your life in many ways – it controls what you wear, the kind of things you eat and even the things you are able to do. You can usually plan ahead, at least a day or so, because of fairly accurate weather forecasts. But there is still little anyone can do to control the weather.

Ancient times

In ancient times the weather was thought to have magical or religous powers. People prayed to the gods for sun and rain to help make their crops grow. The ancient Greeks, for example, had weather gods, such as Zephyrus, god of the west wind and Boreas, god of the north wind. Even today, American Indians, some African tribes and Australian aborigines have tribal "rain makers" who perform ceremonies to make the rains come.

A rain dance.

Bad weather

The weather can affect the way people behave. Teachers often think that children, for example, are bad-tempered when it is very windy. In France, it is even said that the Mistral wind can make people go mad! Riots too, are thought to be more likely to happen when the weather is very hot and humid. Some of Britain's worst riots have happened in this kind of weather.

Feeling low

Many illnesses are made worse by the weather. People with chest ailments suffer more when the air is cold and damp with fog, for instance. Hay fever is a problem in the summer when dry weather helps pollen from flowers and plants fly easily into the air.

Technology beats the weather

Technology sometimes gets round the effects of the weather to enable people to do what they want. For example, ball games such as soccer are played in wet weather – on plastic grass! See how many other examples you can think of where technology beats the weather.

Weather sayings

Weather sayings are simple weather forecasts which have come about over hundreds of years by people watching the weather. Some are still useful today because they are quite accurate.

Mackerel sky and mares' tails, Make tall ships carry low sails. (English saying)

"Mackerel sky" and "mares' tails" describes kinds of clouds which sometimes bring strong winds.

Red sky at night, shepherd's delight, Red sky in the morning, shepherd's warning. (English saying)

This saying means that a sunset is usually followed by a dry night, but rain is on the way if the sky is red in the morning.

A sun shiny shower, Won't last half an hour. (English saying)

Check for yourself if the sun shines during a shower to see if this saying is true.

Christmas on the balcony means Easter in the embers. (French saying)

If it is warm at Christmas, Easter is likely to be cold.

Shelter

All round the world people protect themselves in different ways from the wind, rain, Sun and snow. The weather affects the clothes you need to wear, the kind of house you live in, and even the kind of car you have.

Clothes

The picture on the right shows clothes you might wear in winter or summer. Your body is always trying to keep you at an even temperature. Clothes help by protecting you from the weather.

Your body protects itself too. If you are cold your muscles twitch and make you shiver to keep warm. If you are hot sweat on your skin dries and cools you down.

Winter

- Umbrellas are a simple way of keeping dry.
- A quilted coat traps air inside to keep you warm.
- More heat escapes through your head than any other part of your body.
- Your hands and feet lose heat quickly. Gloves and thick socks in your boots help to protect them.
- Wellington boots were named after the Duke of Wellington, who wore long black boots.

Summer

- The Sun sends out rays. Some of these can be harmful, but there are ways of protecting yourself from them.
- A hat helps to keep the Sun's rays from your head. Too much heat on your head can make you ill.
- Sunglasses cut down the Sun's glare.
- A loose skirt and shorts trap cool air inside them.
- Suntan oil protects your skin from the Sun's harmful rays.

Houses

People have found ways of making their homes comfortable whatever the weather is like. The shape of your home and the things used to build it are all affected by the kind of weather where you live.

The Bahktiari people in Iran stretch their tents over low stone walls. The wind blows through the sides to keep them cool.

Houses in many hot countries are painted white to reflect the Sun's heat and keep them cool.

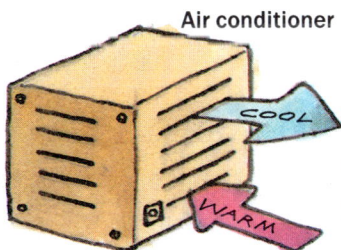

Air conditioner

COOL

WARM

Some people keep their homes cool with a machine called an air-conditioner. This cools the air as it sucks it in from outside.

Loft insulation helps stop heat from escaping upwards.

Double glazing helps stop heat from escaping through the windows.

Homes in Europe and the USA are protected from the cold by trapping warm air inside. This is called insulation.

Cars

Anti-freeze liquid

In cold countries cars need special liquid in the radiator to stop the water inside freezing in winter. Hot-air heaters keep the passengers warm.

Cars in hot countries need special filters to keep dust out of the engine. A filter is a bit like a sieve. Air-conditioners keep the car cool inside.

Wildlife and the weather

The weather affects animals in many different ways. Some animals, like hedgehogs, go to sleep for the whole winter to escape the cold. Others, like lizards, need the warmth of the Sun to make their bodies work. Farmers especially have to pay attention to the weather to make sure their animals are well protected.

Winter sleep

Some animals find life difficult in the winter. There is very little food around, so animals such as hedgehogs, tortoises and doormice, eat as much as possible in the autumn. They live off their fat by sleeping for the whole winter in a warm place. This is called hibernating.

A hibernating animal's temperature drops to match its surroundings and its heart beat slows right down to save energy.

When it is frozen, birds such as robins cannot dig their beaks into the ground to find worms and insects to eat.

Hill farmers often lose sheep in deep snow drifts. Sheep, like the one in the picture above, manage to stay alive for days under the snow until they are dug out.

Birds find it difficult to get a drink when it is icy because they cannot peck through the ice. It is a good idea to leave a dish of warm water out for them.

Hibernating hedgehog

In harsh winters, such as in 1987, helicopters are used to airlift food to horses and cattle stranded in remote areas.

Fly away

Some birds fly away to warmer places in the winter. This is called migrating.

In December or January, Gulls, Lapwings, Woodpigeons, Robins, Thrushes and Starlings fly to Britain if it is very cold in Norway, Sweden and Denmark.

Swifts, Swallows and Cuckoos fly to Africa each autumn and return after the winter. They migrate whatever the weather is like.

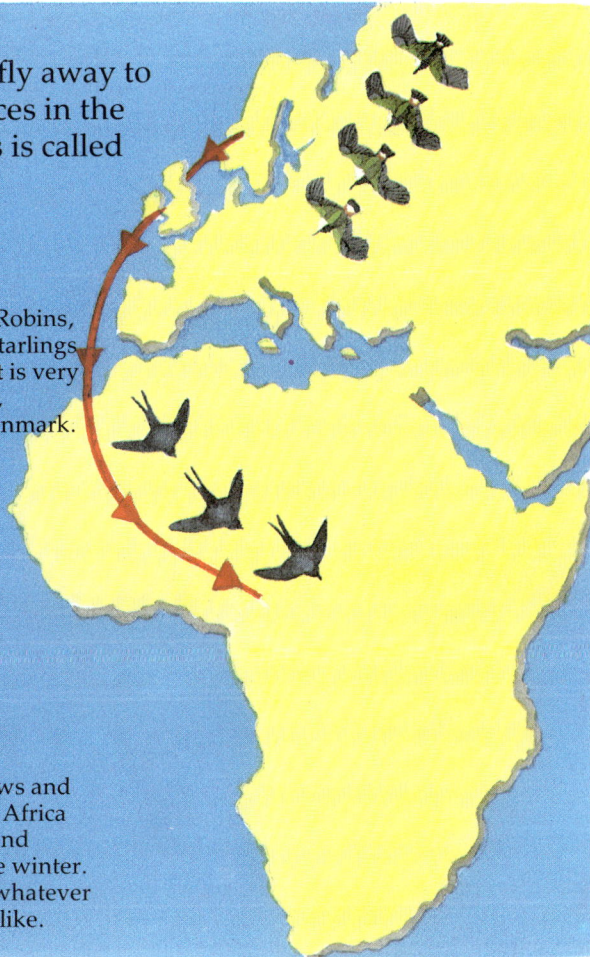

Animal migration

Animals as well as birds need to migrate. Waterbucks in Southern Africa, for example, migrate to wetter areas during the dry season.

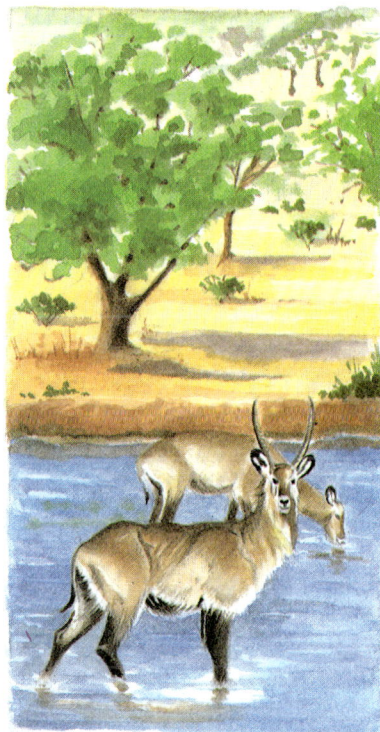

Hot dog

On a hot day, you will see dogs panting. Dogs cannot cool down by sweating, but lose heat through their tongues instead.

Lizards

Lizards and other reptiles are cold-blooded. They need heat from the Sun to warm up. When it is cold they are not very active.

Wet birds

Birds hide in hedges and under bushes when it rains. They keep warm by puffing up their feathers to insulate themselves.

Climate

Each area of the earth has a certain kind of weather, from scorched deserts and steamy rainforests to lush pastures and fertile valleys. The pattern of weather these places expect from year to year is called their climate. Some places, such as the Antarctic, have very extreme climates – the temperature there is below freezing even in summer. Other places, such as Britain, have very mild climates because the weather is neither very hot nor very cold.

Different climates

The world is divided into different types of climate, shown on the map below. The climate depends on how far somewhere is from the equator. This distance is called latitude and is measured in degrees. Climate also depends how far somewhere is from the sea and on its position on a continent.

Tropical grasslands and monsoons: very wet or very dry.

Polar: cold, ice-covered lands, some snow in the Antarctic, but less in the Arctic.

Temperate: changeable weather, usually with warm, dry summers and mild winters.

Desert: very little or no rainfall. Little variation in weather between the seasons.

Mountain: colder the higher up you go.

Cold forest: very cold in winter, hot in summer.

Rainforest: hot and wet all year round.

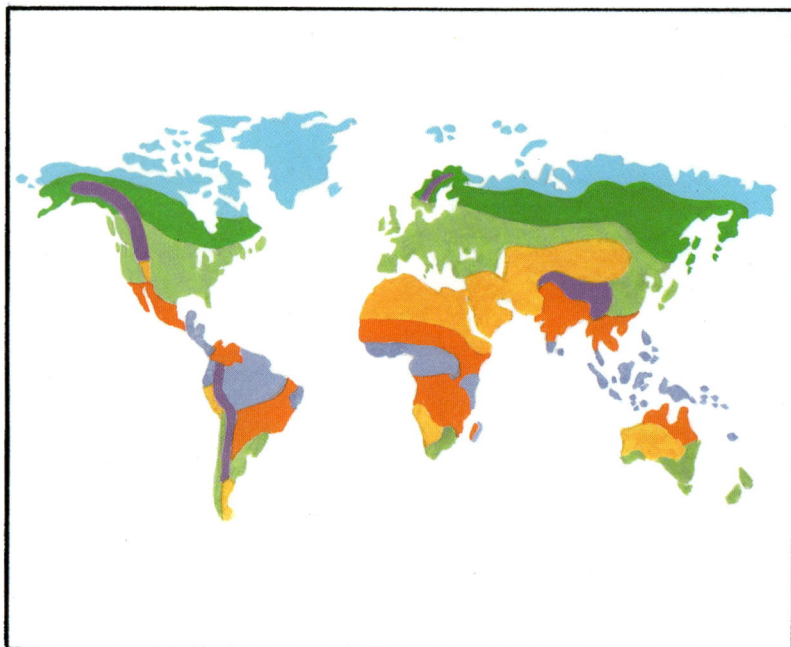

Odd climates?

Moscow and Edinburgh are on the same latitude, but the climate is very different. This is because Edinburgh is near the sea, while Moscow is hundreds of kilometres from it. Places near the coast are called maritime climates. Here, the temperatures stay fairly even through the year because the sea temperature does not vary much.

Edinburgh is warm in summer and mild in winter.

Moscow is very hot in summer and freezing cold in winter.

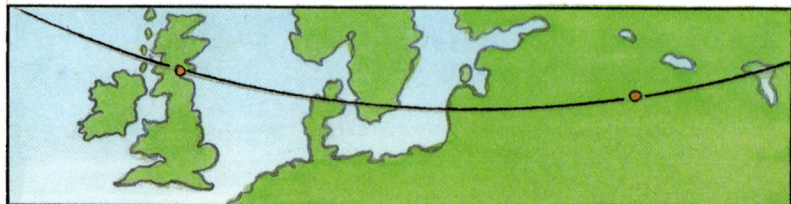

Country climates

ATLANTIC OCEAN

The Pyrenees get lots of snow in winter because they are so high. You can go skiing here.

Corunna has a fairly wet climate because it is affected by weather from the north.

Corunna

SPAIN

Mountains

Winds blow from the west in winter and bring rain.

MEDITERRANEAN

Madrid

Mountains

Lisbon has changeable weather because of the winds blowing across the Atlantic.

PORTUGAL

Lisbon

Madrid is high up and is cold in winter and hot in summer.

Seville is the hottest place in Europe during the summer.

Benidorm

This part of the coast is sheltered by mountains from the rainy winds blowing from the west in winter.

Seville

Torremolinos
Marbella

Mountains, the sea and the general wind direction, all affect the climate within a small area. The climate in Spain and Portugal, for example, varies from place to place.

Microclimates

Scientists call the climate in very small areas a microclimate. A microclimate can be the size of a city or as small as a back garden! The examples below show how different the climate can be even within a tiny area. This affects the kind of plants that grow, or the sort of animals you find.

Gardens

In Britain, south-facing walls are the warmest spot in a garden because they are sheltered and get the sun all day as it passes from east to west.

Mountains and hills

The bottoms of valleys are always protected from strong winds, but can be in the cold shadow of the surrounding hills. Hilltops are exposed to strong winds, making it difficult for trees to grow.

Cities

Cities are often much warmer than the surrounding countryside. All the concrete stores the Sun's heat during the day, warming the air at night.

Hot and cold

Whether you feel hot or cold depends on lots of things – the strength of the wind or the clothes you are wearing, for example – but most of all it depends on the amount of heat from the Sun. The warmth you feel is called the temperature.

Day and night

The Earth spins round once every 24 hours. Daytime is where the Sun is shining onto the planet. The Earth absorbs energy from the Sun and gives it out as heat. Much of the heat you feel actually comes from the Earth and not the Sun.

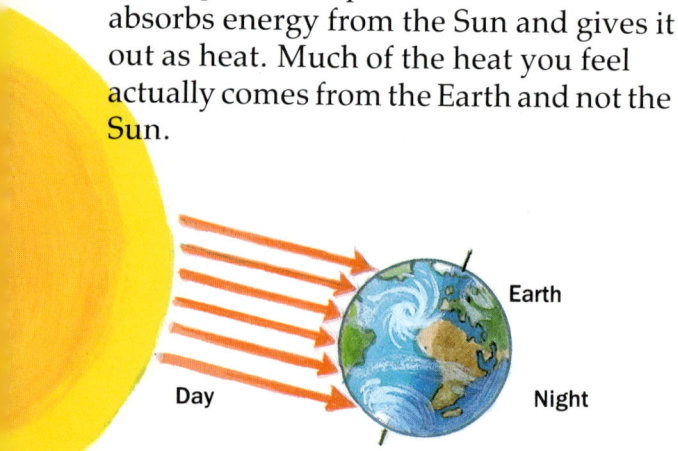

Earth

Day   Night

The Sun warms the surface during the day. It starts to get cooler at sunset.

At night, the surface gradually loses its warmth. The coldest time is at dawn, just before this side turns to face the sun again.

Sunsets

A sunset happens when the Sun goes behind a hill or a mountain as the Earth spins. Sometimes you can see the Sun shining on a cloud after it has gone down.

Why are the poles cold?

The Sun's rays hit the Earth in straight lines, as shown in the picture. Because the surface is curved, the rays spread out more at the poles than they do at the equator. This makes the poles much colder than the equator.

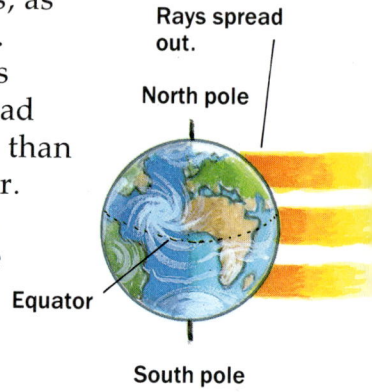

Rays spread out.

North pole

Equator

South pole

Measuring the temperature

Temperature is measured with a thermometer in units called degrees Centigrade or Celsius. A small bulb at the bottom contains a liquid which expands, or gets bigger, as it gets warmer. The liquid is forced up the glass tube and you can read the temperature marked beside it on a scale.

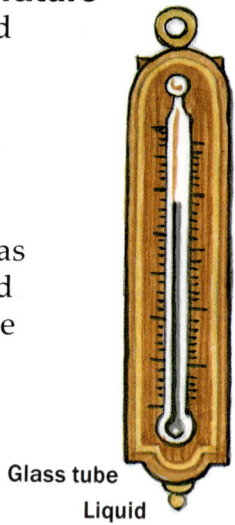

Glass tube

Liquid

A Swedish man called Anders Celsius introduced the Centigrade scale (°C) in 1742. Gabriel Daniel Fahrenheit of Germany invented the Fahrenheit scale (°F) in 1718.

The seasons

The Earth takes one year to go round the Sun. The seasons of spring, summer, autumn and winter are caused by different parts of the Earth being tilted towards the Sun as the Earth goes round.

Summer in the northern hemisphere.

Winter in the northern hemisphere.

Winter in the southern hemisphere.

Summer in the southern hemisphere.

The North Pole is tilted towards the Sun.

The North Pole is tilted away from the Sun.

Hottest place on Earth

The hottest place on Earth is Dallol in Ethiopia. The average temperature in the shade is 34.4°C.

Coldest place on Earth

Vostok, near the South Pole, is very cold. The temperature is often minus 70°C. Even a home freezer is much warmer!

Pressure

The weight of all the air in the atmosphere pressing down on everything is called air pressure. The pressure varies constantly from place to place, getting higher or lower, and bringing different kinds of weather.

High pressure areas usually have settled and sunny weather, while low pressure brings clouds and rain. The differences in pressure also decide which way the wind will blow.

The weight of air

An Italian, called Evangelista Torricelli, first discovered that air had weight in 1604. Try this simple experiment to prove that air weighs something. Tie two balloons to a stick as shown in the picture, then pop one of them with a pin. What happens to the other balloon? Can you think why?

Blow up the balloons so that they are about the same size.

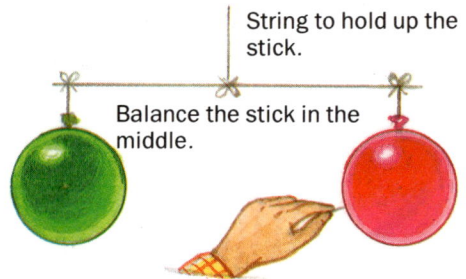

String to hold up the stick.

Balance the stick in the middle.

Pressure and height

Air pressure gets lower the higher up you go. The pressure at the top of a mountain or around an aircraft, for example, is much lower than at sea level. The picture below shows why this happens. The top cylinder stays round, but the others get more and more squashed by the weight of the others above.

Make six paper cylinders and push them onto a knitting needle.

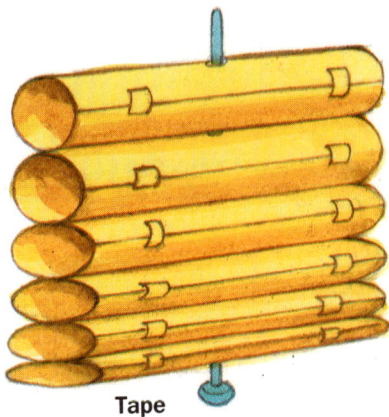

Tape

Air pressure varies at different heights because of the weight of air pressing down.

Aircraft cabins are specially pressurized so that people are safe inside.

There is less oxygen to breathe the higher up you go.

The air pressure at sea level is just over 1kg per square centimetre. Imagine a bag of sugar pressing down on every square centimetre of your body to get an idea of how much the air above you weighs. You don't feel this weight because the air inside your body balances the pressure on the outside.

Hot air

Air pressure not only changes with height, but with temperature too. The warmer it gets, the less air there is. This affects the pressure. Some areas of Earth get hotter than others, so there are different areas of high and low pressure – and these are constantly changing.

More heat from the Sun reaches areas of the earth clear of cloud. This changes the temperature and the pressure in that area.

The temperature over the sea is warmer than the land in winter, but colder in summer. This makes the pressure vary between land and sea.

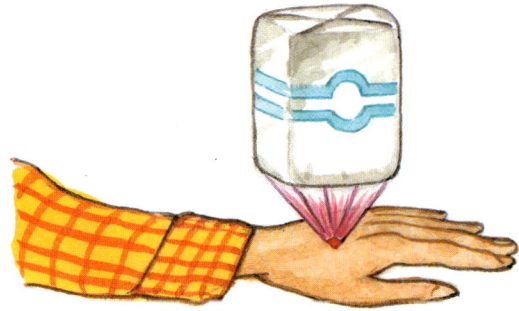

Highs and lows

Weather forecasters gather measurements from all round the world and make maps of the pressure areas. These are called highs and lows. Highs are areas where the pressure gets higher towards the centre, and lows are where it gets lower. If you stand with your back to the wind, the nearest low is on the left in the northern hemisphere and on the right in the southern.

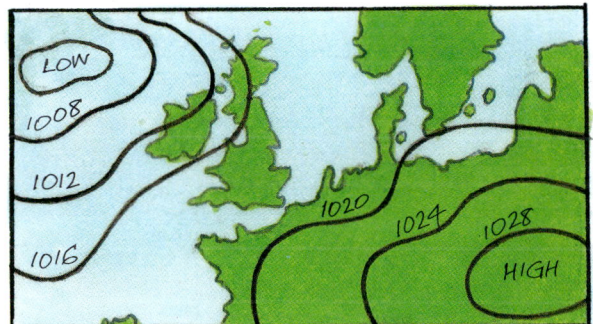

The lines on these maps are called isobars. The pressure is the same all along the line. The numbers on the map show the amount of pressure.

Barometers

Pressure is measured in units called millibars with a barometer. If you have one at home you can tell if a high is on the way when the pressure starts to rise, or a low if it falls.

See how to make a barometer on page 135.

Wind

The air around the Earth is always moving – across the surface of the planet and up and down too. Wind is air moving from one place to another. Sometimes you can tell where the wind has come from. Strong winds from the Sahara desert, for example, sometimes pick up dust and blow it thousands of kilometers to Europe. The dust is often left on cars and even colours the snow in the Alps.

What makes the wind blow?

A constant movement of warm and cold air makes the wind blow. The heat from the sun warms up different parts of the sea and land. These in turn warm the air above them. Air that is warmed becomes lighter than the surrounding air, so it rises. In other places, the air cools. Cold air becomes heavier, so it sinks. The wind blows because the cold air moves to replace the warmer air.

Masses of air

There are huge areas of air, called air masses. They are warm, cold, dry or moist depending on the land or sea they pass over. Boundaries between air masses are called fronts. There is usually wet, cloudy-weather where cold and warm fronts occur.

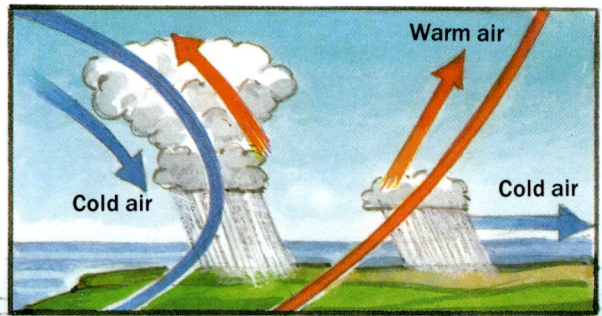

Air in a heated room circulates in the same way as the wind moves.

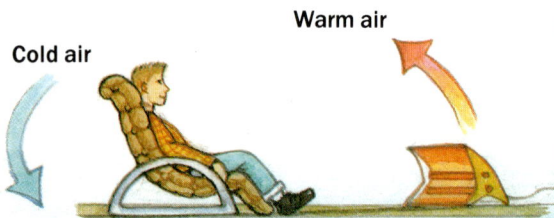

Warm air

Cold air

Warm air

Cold air

Cold air

Wind direction

You can see the direction of the wind by looking at a weather vane on a tower or church. A weather vane is made to point in the direction from which the wind blows. Wind direction is always given by saying the compass point from which it is blowing.

A wind sock is used at airfields to show the direction and strength of the wind.

A south wind blows from the south to the north.

An east wind blows from the east to the west.

A north wind blows from the north to the south.

A west wind blows from the west to the east.

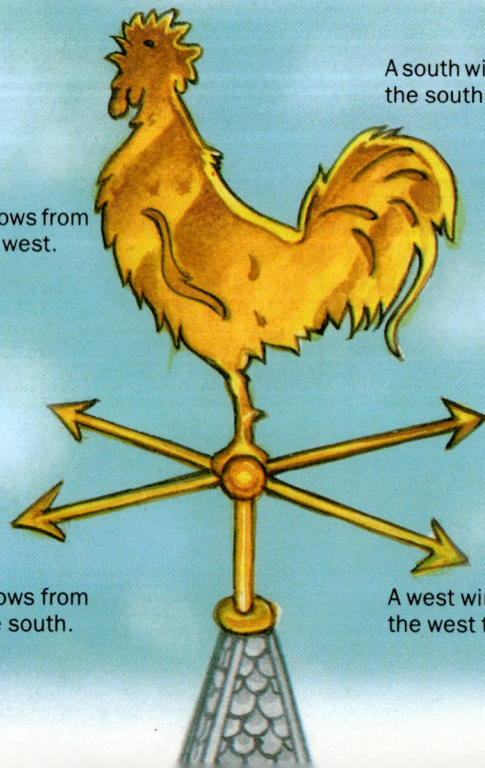

Wind speed

In 1805, Admiral Sir Francis Beaufort worked out a scale for measuring wind speed at sea. His scale is still used today, but has been altered for use on land.

Force 1 (2-5kph)
Light air

Smoke drifts but wind vanes do not move.

Force 2 (6-11kph)
Light breeze

Leaves rustle and wind vanes move.

Force 3 (12-19kph)
Gentle breeze

Leaves and small twigs move.

Force 4 (20-29kph)
Moderate breeze

Dust raised, small branches move.

Force 5 (30-39kph)
Fresh breeze

Small trees with leaves sway.

Force 6 (40-50kph)
Strong breeze

Large branches move. Phone wires whistle.

Force 7 (51-61kph)
Near gale

Whole trees sway.

Force 8 (62-74kph)
Gale

Twigs break off trees. Walking difficult.

Force 9 (75-87kph)
Strong gale

Chimney pots brought down.

Force 10 (88-102kph)
Storm

Damage to buildings. Trees uprooted.

Force 11 (103-120kph)
Violent storm

Widespread damage.

Force 12 (over 120kph)
Hurricane

Whole area devastated.

Beach breezes

Winds often begin near the sea. You can feel this sometimes when a cool breeze blows from the sea to the beach. On a hot summer day, the land warms up more quickly than the sea. Air above the land rises, so cooler air from the sea blows in to replace it. The wind blows in the opposite direction at night because the land cools more quickly than the sea.

Using the wind

People used to use the wind to power windmills, but in most countries today it is more often used to turn giant propellors to generate electricity.

Windmill still in use in Greece.

What is a cloud

Clouds are made up of billions of tiny droplets of ice or water. Being in a cloud would be just like being in fog. In fact, fog is a cloud formed near the ground.

Each cloud droplet is smaller than a speck of flour. The droplets are so small and light that they fall slowly enough for the air to hold them up.

How clouds are made

Clouds are condensation, formed when warm air rises and is cooled below a certain temperature, called its dew point. This happens in the same way to condensation forming on a window or a mirror in the bathroom.

Clouds of dust

Water droplets in a cloud float much like dust. You can see this effect by closing the curtains in a room on a sunny day and letting a shaft of light shine through.

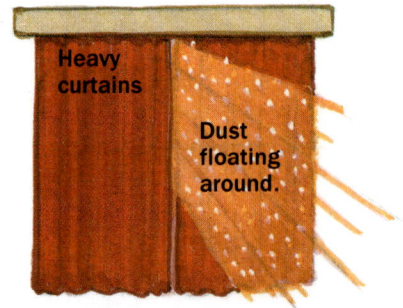

Warm air cools on the cold glass and condenses to form water droplets.

Heavy curtains

Dust floating around.

Flying through clouds

Pilots often fly right through the clouds to bright sunshine above. This picture shows cumulus clouds from a plane window.

Ten cloud types

There are three basic families of clouds, called cirrus ("curl of hair"), stratus ("layer") and cumulus ("heap"). They were given these Latin names by Luke Howard in 1804. There are seven other main types of clouds made up of combinations of these families. The kind of clouds you see give clues about the weather.

Clouds

Cirrus
Stratus
Cumulus
Cirrostratus
Altostratus
Nimbostratus
Stratocumulus
Cirrocumulus
Altocumulus
Cumulonimbus

See if you can identify these clouds:

Cirrus

Stratus

Cumulus

Cirrus are thin clouds, often called "mares' tails". After fine weather, they may show stormy weather on the way.

Stratus is a low grey blanket of cloud which often brings drizzle. They often cover high ground and cause fog.

These clouds look like giant puffs of cotton wool. Each may hold 1,000 tonnes of water – the same as 200 fully grown elephants.

Cumulonimbus are the most impressive clouds. They tower up to 15km high, almost twice as high as Mount Everest. Often they contain over half a million tonnes of water – enough to fill 250 million buckets! They are a sure sign of rain, but not necessarily over you.

These clouds often look like a giant anvil.

Cumulonimbus means "heaped rain cloud".

Why different clouds?

Different sorts of clouds are formed because air rises for different reasons.

Air can be warmed by a small area of ground – fields heat more quickly than forests, for example. The air rises, cools and condenses to form a cumulus cloud. This process is called convection.

When air is blown against a hill it is forced to rise over the top. Often, this cools the air enough to form a cloud.

If a large amount of cold air meets warm air, it flows under the warm air and forces it upwards. This often forms stratus clouds.

Why does it rain?

Three main things are needed to make rain: plenty of moisture in the atmosphere, deep clouds (such as cumulonimbus or nimbostratus) and rising air. The word precipitation is sometimes used for rain, snow or drizzle.

How it rains

Scientists think that tiny water droplets in the cloud stick to floating particles of dust or salt.

The water droplets are constantly moving. They bump into each other and gradually get bigger.

Larger droplets start to fall, gathering smaller ones on the way, gradually growing bigger and falling faster.

As the raindrop falls, its shape is like an orange flattened at the bottom and not like a tear-drop, as many people imagine.

Raindrops

Surface tension

You can see the surface tension of water if you fill a glass almost to overflowing.

A raindrop can be up to about 8mm in diameter – the size of a pea. The raindrop is held together by its surface tension. This is like a "skin" on the water. The surface tension breaks above this size and smaller drops are formed.

Measuring the rain

Rainfall is measured with an instrument called a rain gauge. They have been used since the 15th century to keep records of the amount of rainfall each day. The simplest sort is a funnel in a marked container. The pictures below show how to make your own.

1
Pour water to a depth of 20mm in a wide jar.

2
Pour the water into a narrow jar. It will come much higher up.

3
Tape a piece of paper to the jar and mark off ten equal divisions.

4
Fix a funnel in the jar, sealing it with Plasticene.

5
Place above grass level so water will not splash in and affect your readings.

Read measurements in millimetres.

Showers and rain

Sometimes it pours for hours, but at other times there is just a quick shower. Air rising slowly over a large area will make it rain for several hours, but when the air rushes upwards over a small area there will only be a shower. The picture below shows how long rain or showers will last.

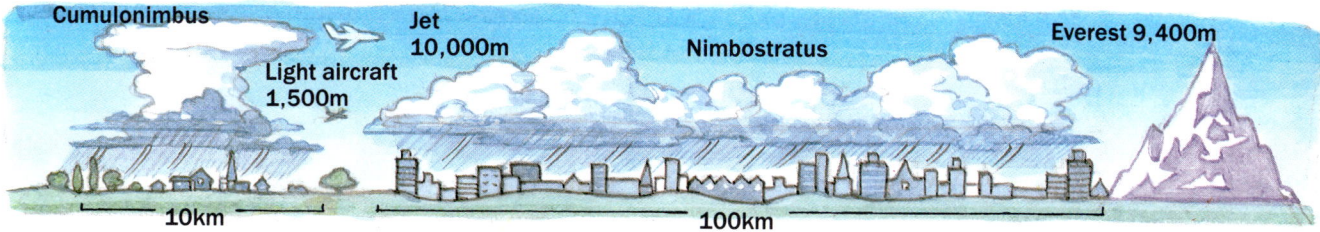

Cumulonimbus · Light aircraft 1,500m · Jet 10,000m · Nimbostratus · Everest 9,400m · 10km · 100km

The cloud passes at 20kph, so the shower lasts for 30 minutes over the village.

The cloud passes at 20kph, so the rain lasts for 5 hours over the town.

The importance of rain

People need rain for drinking water, for their animals and for growing crops. Terrible droughts, caused by a lack of rain, strike many areas of the world each year.

Drought in Ethiopia in the early 1980's caused famine amongst millions of people.

The water cycle

Water is constantly on the move in a process called the water cycle. The same water goes round the cycle over and over again.

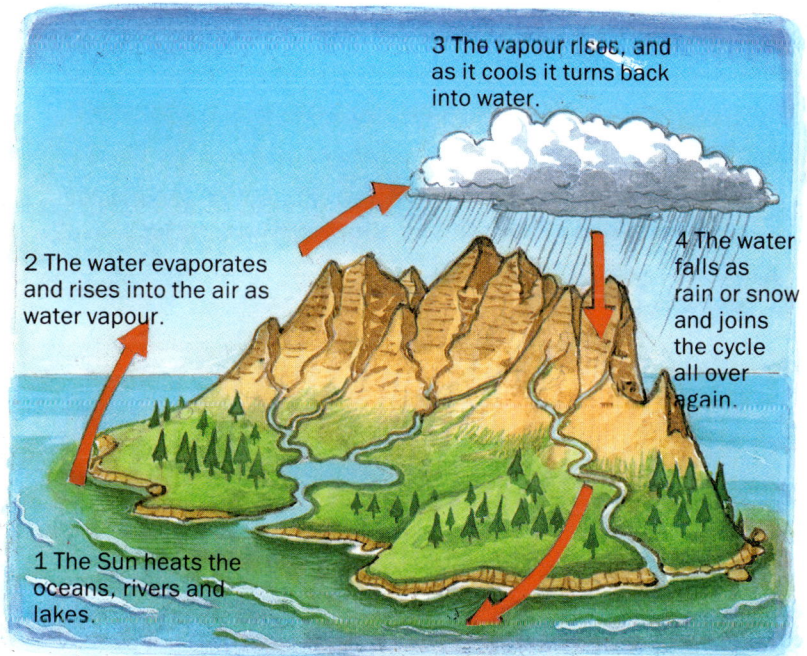

3 The vapour rises, and as it cools it turns back into water.

2 The water evaporates and rises into the air as water vapour.

4 The water falls as rain or snow and joins the cycle all over again.

1 The Sun heats the oceans, rivers and lakes.

GREATEST RAINFALLS			LEAST RAINFALLS		
Continent	mm each year	place	Continent	mm each year	place
Oceania	11,684	Mt Wai-'ale-'ale, Hawaii	S. America	0.8	Arica, Chile
Asia	11,430	Cherrapunji, India	Africa	2.5	Wadi Halfa, Sudan
Africa	10,277	Debundseha, Cameroon	N. America	30.5	Bataques, Mexico
S. America	8,991	Quibdo, Colombia	Asia	45.7	Aden, South Yemen
N. America	6,655	Henderson Lake, British Columbia	Australia	119.3	Millers Creek
Europe	4,648	Grkvice, Yugoslavia	Europe	160.0	Cabo de Gata, Spain
Australia	4,496	Tully, Queensland	Oceania	226.0	Puako, Hawaii

Thunder and lightning

Thunderstorms happen when large amounts of warm moist air move upwards very quickly – often on a summer afternoon. You can see a storm forming when cumulus clouds grow quickly into cumulonimbus clouds, the skies darken and the wind starts to blow. A thunderstorm, with heavy rain, thunder and lightning, will often only last for an hour or so. Each day there are thousands of them raging somewhere around the Earth!

Warm air moving upwards very quickly – a storm starts to form.

What causes lightning?

Violent air currents blow up and down inside a cumulonimbus cloud, forcing water droplets and ice crystals to crash into each other. Scientists think this creates friction between all the particles, causing static electricity. Each water droplet in the cloud is charged with either positive or negative electricity.

Sheet lightning

You see sheet lightning as a glow in the clouds. This is caused by sparks jumping between the positive and negative charges within the cloud.

Positive charges of electricity build up at the top of the cloud, negative charges at the bottom.

The ground is charged with positive electricity. There is an electrical "gap" between the cloud and the ground.

What is static electricity?

This is called the leader stroke.

The difference between the positive and negative charges gets bigger and bigger, until a spark jumps the gap.

Another stroke returns from the ground to the cloud. Both strokes happen so quickly that you see them as one.

Static electricity is electricity at rest, waiting to move. You can create it by rubbing a balloon on synthetic fabric. The electric charge will make the balloon stick to a wall. Try this in the dark and you may see sparks of electricity jump from the balloon to the wall.

What is thunder?

Lightning heats the air in its path to 30,000°C – five times hotter than the Sun's surface. The air expands and moves faster than the speed of sound, causing the crashing noise of thunder. Thunder and lightning happen at the same time, but light travels faster than sound, so you see the flash before you hear the thunderclap.

Sound travels at 330m per second

Light travels at 300,000km per second.

If you hear the thunder three seconds after you see the flash, the storm is about 1km away.

Crazy experiment

In an 18th century storm, Benjamin Franklin flew a kite dangling a metal key. He wanted to prove that there was electricity in storms, but his experiment was very dangerous because electricity is attracted to metal. He invented the lightning conductor in 1752.

Am I safe?

Buildings are sometimes damaged and people injured or killed by lightning. Lightning takes the shortest and quickest path to the ground, usually to a high object standing alone.

Lightning strikes aircraft, but the people inside are safe because it runs round the outside.

Lightning strikes lone trees on high ground – don't shelter here!

If you get stuck in the open, make yourself low by crouching down or run for shelter.

You are safe inside a car. The electricity is carried to the ground through the tyres.

You are safe indoors.

Lightning strikes tall buildings, but they have a copper strip called a lightning conductor to carry the electricity harmlessly to the ground. The Empire State Building in New York has been struck by lightning as much as 48 times in one day!

Dew, mist, fog and frost

Dew, mist, fog and frost are all the result of water vapour being in the air, cooling down and condensing (turning back to water or ice). There is always moisture, or water vapour, in the air – even in deserts. You can see the water vapour in your own breath condense on a cold day, as clouds of "steam" as you breathe out.

Wet air

The warmer the air, the more moisture it can hold. At 20°C, for example, the air can hold four times as much water vapour as air at 0°C. The air in a small bedroom might hold about a cupful of water.

The dew point

Air is a bit like a sponge. A sponge in a bowl of water will soak up the water until it can hold no more. Saturated air can hold no more water vapour. The temperature at which this happens is called the dew point. If the temperature drops below this point, the excess water vapour condenses to form water droplets.

Dew

On a calm, clear night, heat escapes quickly from the earth and air close to the ground cools below its dew point. The water vapour in the air condenses onto cold surfaces, such as grass, plants and cobwebs, and forms dew. The dew evaporates, or turns back to water vapour, as the air warms during the day.

Mist and fog

Condensation in the air near the ground forms mist or fog. This often happens in the evening as the ground is cooling. The cool air is heavier than the warmer air above, so the mist tends to gather near the ground or in valleys. To weather forecasters, mist becomes fog when they cannot see anything more than 1km away.

Contrails

Have you ever wondered about the white trails left in the sky by jets? These are called contrails and are caused by burnt jet fuel, which includes water vapour, condensing and freezing into ice crystals. This usually happens if the jet is flying above 10,000m.

Rime

The water droplets in fog sometimes freeze when they touch cold objects, such as trees and power lines. This is called rime.

Frost

If dew freezes after it has settled, it is called hoar frost. This makes beautiful fern-like patterns on windows. Frost can also form directly if the ground is already below 0°C.

Smog

Smog like this was called a "pea-souper".

1950s

Today

Many cities of the world have terrible smog. Smog is a mixture of fog and smoke particles. The pictures above show what London was like before smokeless fuels were introduced.

Ice and snow

Water freezes to ice when its temperature drops below 0°C. Ponds freeze over and roads become very dangerous. Black ice is even worse. This name is given to ice that you can hardly see on the road. It can be caused when it rains and freezes soon afterwards.

Trucks cover icy roads at night with salt to melt the ice. Most of the salt comes from Cheshire or Germany.

Ice experiment

As it freezes, water expands by about 9%. Water pipes burst in winter because the ice splits the pipe. This experiment shows what happens:

1 Fill a plastic bottle to the brim and replace the cap.

2 Put the bottle in a freezer for a few hours.

3 The bottle will have split when you take it out.

Don't use a glass bottle.

Icebergs

Icebergs are giant slabs of ice that break away from the polar ice caps in warm weather. They float because ice is lighter than water. In the early 1980's scientists planned to tow an iceberg to Saudi Arabia and Kuwait to use for drinking water, but the plan was abandoned.

The most famous iceberg was one which sank the SS Titanic in 1912.

Most of the salt in sea water stays in the sea when it freezes.

Only about 10% of an iceberg is visible above the water.

Hailstones

Hail only falls from cumulonimbus clouds. Particles of ice are blown up and down inside the cloud, gradually getting bigger as they collect more layers of ice on the way. Eventually the hailstone drops out of the cloud.

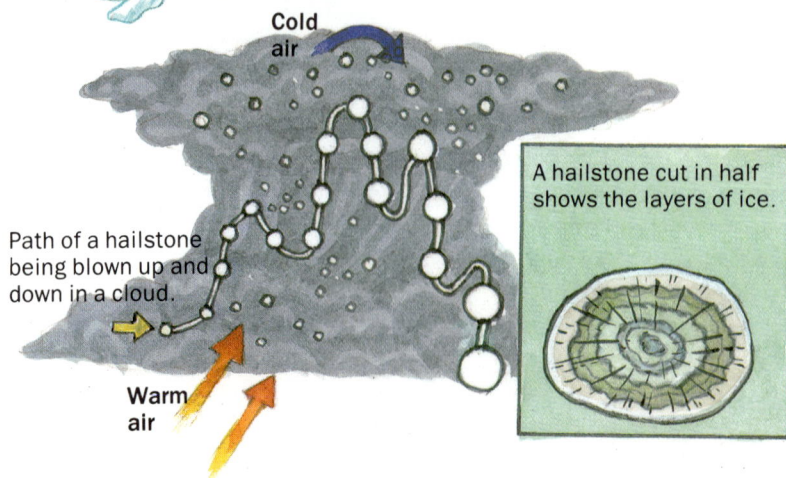

Cold air

Path of a hailstone being blown up and down in a cloud.

Warm air

A hailstone cut in half shows the layers of ice.

Snow

Snow crystals are formed in a cloud where the temperature is well below freezing point. They are made by water freezing onto ice particles. As a crystal falls through the cloud it hits others and becomes a snowflake. The air has to be below freezing too, or the snowflake will melt and turn to rain.

Flake shapes

Snow flakes are always six-sided and no two are ever alike. Their shape depends on the temperature – needle and rod shapes are made in colder air, while more complex shapes are made in warmer air.

You can collect snow flakes to look at under a hand lens on a piece of black paper.

Different snow flake patterns.

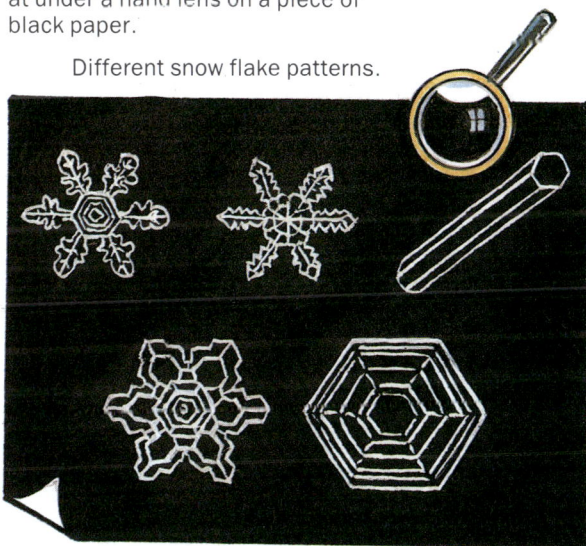

Avalanche!

An avalanche is when thousands of tonnes of snow fall from the side of a mountain, crashing into the valley below. An avalanche can be started by skiers, a thaw in the snow, a strong wind, or a heavy fall of fresh snow sliding across old snow.

Old ice

Scientists can find out about past weather by drilling holes in glaciers and pulling out long plugs of ice. The plugs are layered and they can tell how cold the weather was by testing each layer.

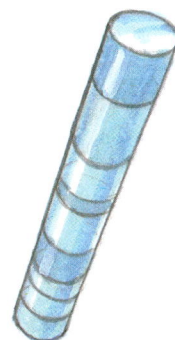

Snow experiment

Fill ten empty yogurt pots with fresh snow without squashing it down too much. Let it melt indoors and see if you can work out how much snow you need to make one yogurt pot full of water.

Answer: About 10 yogurt pots of snow make one pot of water.

Snow drifts

Snow can get very deep by being blown into drifts by the wind. In 1917 there were 25m drifts in parts of Ireland – deep enough to cover a six storey building!

Trees are specially planted to help stop the snow in its tracks.

Hurricanes and tornadoes

Hurricanes are incredibly destructive storms which usually begin over warm parts of the world's oceans. A hurricane generates as much energy in one second as ten atomic bombs. The wind is strong enough to demolish houses and whip up vast waves which destroy boats and harbours. Hurricanes last between two and five days and are called different things in each area, as you can see on the map on the right.

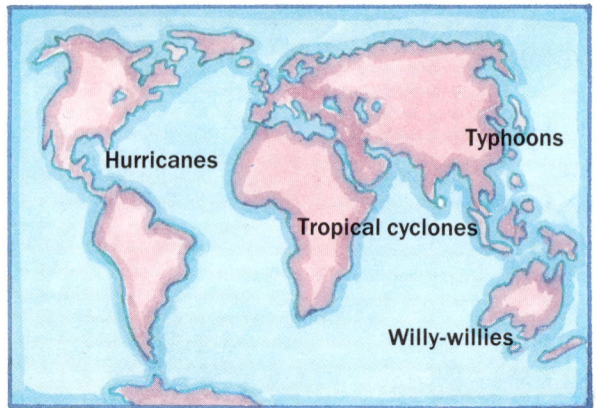

How a hurricane is formed

1 Winds going in opposite directions meet over the sea where heat from the Sun evaporates huge amounts of water.

2 The warm air rises and more air rushes in to take its place. It goes around and up in a spiral.

3 Gradually, the wind blows faster and faster until it reaches anything between 118kph and 320kph.

4 The hurricane moves westwards and is usually about 300km across. Some hurricanes never reach land.

Hurricane names

When a hurricane is spotted it is given a name to identify it. The first of the season begins with an "A", the next a "B" and so on. This was first done in the last century by Clement Wragge, an Australian weather forecaster.

Worst hurricane

The worst hurricane was in Bangladesh in 1970, when about one million people were killed by flooding. In 1975, the city of Darwin, Australia was flattened by Hurricane Tracey.

Hurricane hits Britain

On 16 October 1987, a very severe gale hit southern Britain and northern France, with very little warning. The winds were as strong as a hurricane, between force 10 and 12, but the gale was not a true tropical hurricane.

This is a satellite picture of a hurricane. In the centre is an "eye", where the weather is calm, with light winds and clear skies. There is a lull in the storm as the "eye" passes overhead.

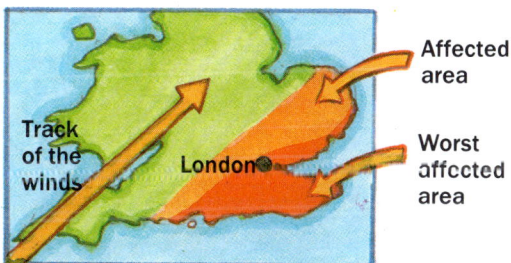

Affected area

Worst affected area

Track of the winds

London

The gale began off the coast of Portugal. Weather forecasters under-estimated the strength of the wind because of a lack of weather reporting ships in the area.

Track of the winds

Portugal

The gale caused massive damage. Over 13 million trees were uprooted, homes were wrecked and without power for days, and cars flattened. Thirteen people were killed. Trees were uprooted because the ground was so wet.

Tornadoes

Tornadoes, or "twisters", form over land and last between 10 minutes and four hours. They are more violent than hurricanes, but much smaller. A tornado is caused by clouds condensing and sucking a funnel of air into the sky. Winds swirl at up to 500kph along a path about 100 metres wide, causing total devastation.

This picture shows a tornado swirling over Australia.

A tornado leapfrogs across the land, sucking up anything in its path when it touches the ground.

Tornadoes are most common in central USA.

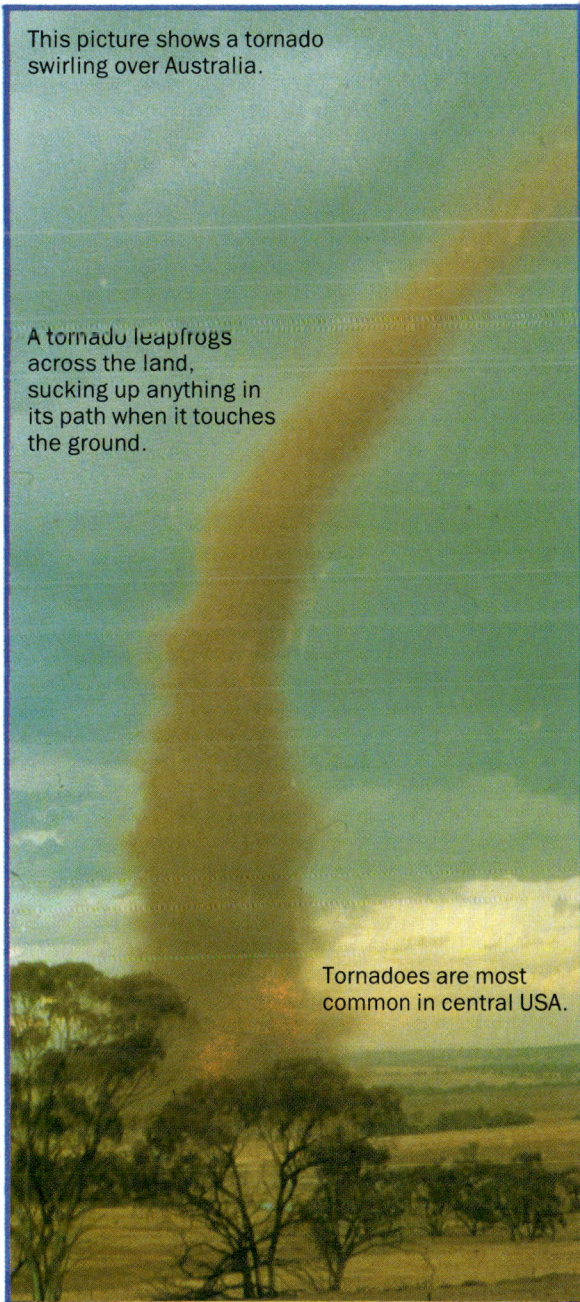

Weather tricks

The weather can cause odd effects, from rainbows to red snow and even hails of fish and crabs falling from the sky! Many effects are common and caused by tricks of the light. Others, like reports in the USA of a tornado picking up a railway engine and turning it round, are unlikely ever to happen again.

Rainbows

Rainbows happen when it is raining and the Sun is shining at the same time. You must have your back to the Sun to see a rainbow. Rainbows form a complete circle, but only part of it is seen from the ground. You can see the whole rainbow in an aircraft, mid-way between the rain cloud and the ground.

Red is on the outside.

Violet is on the inside.

Make a rainbow

You can make a rainbow with a garden spray on a sunny day. Stand with your back to the sun and look through the mist.

About light

Sunlight is made up of seven colours – red, orange, yellow, green, blue, indigo and violet. These are called the colours of the spectrum. Normally, you don't see them individually.

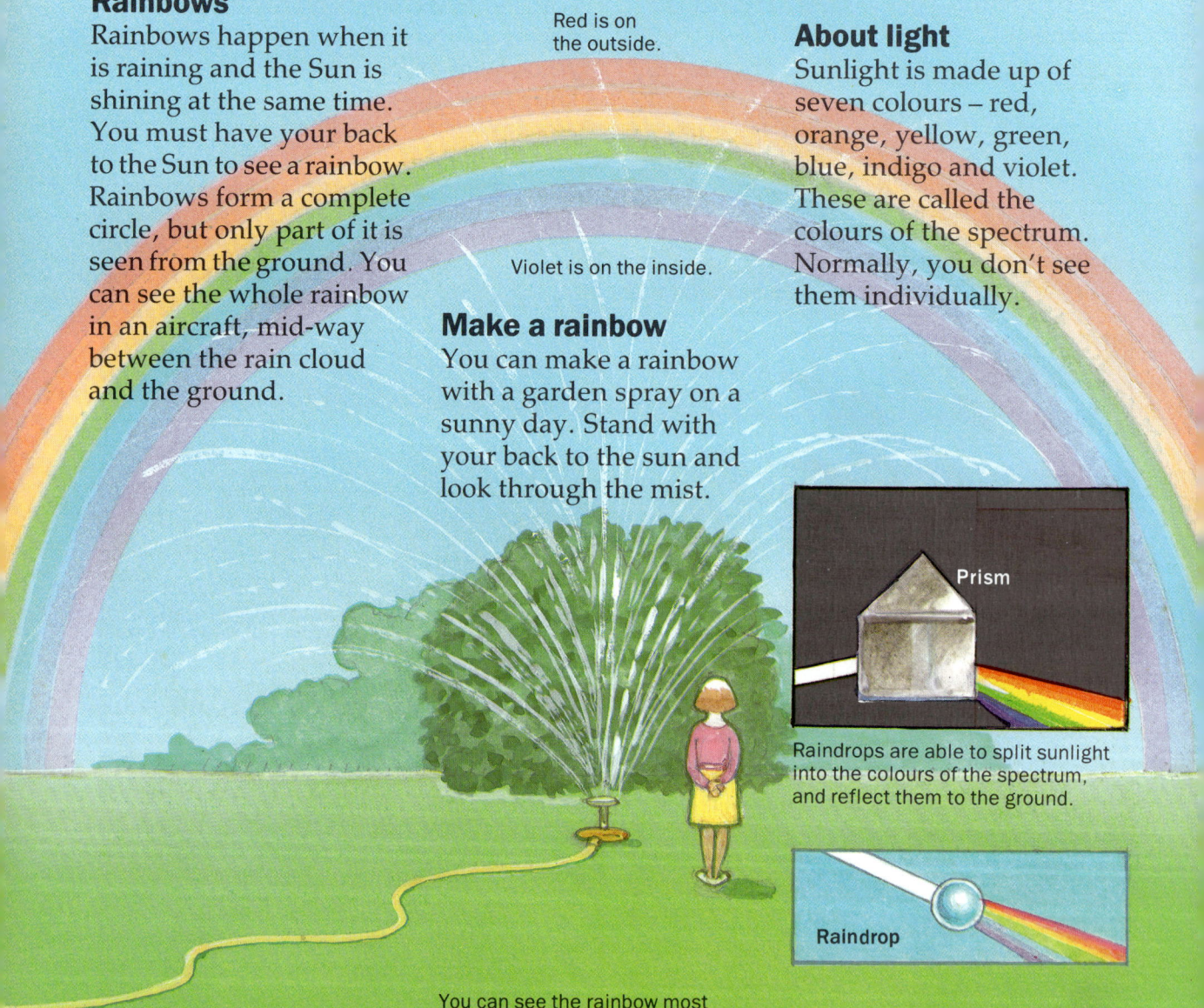

Prism

Raindrops are able to split sunlight into the colours of the spectrum, and reflect them to the ground.

Raindrop

Why is the sky blue?

The Earth's atmosphere contains countless billions of molecules. When rays of sunlight shine through them, some of the blue light from the spectrum is scattered, making the atmosphere look blue.

You can see the rainbow most clearly against a dark-coloured background.

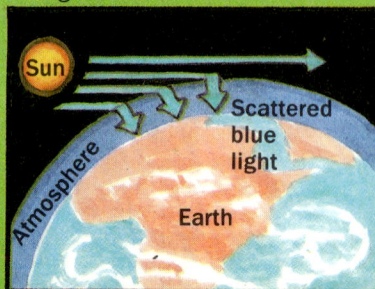

Sun

Scattered blue light

Atmosphere

Earth

If the atmosphere is very polluted, then more of the other colours of the spectrum are scattered. This makes the sky look milky white – often very noticeable over England, Central Europe and northeastern USA.

Haloes

Sometimes, for a few minutes, you can see a halo round the Sun or Moon. You can usually reckon on it raining within a few hours if you see one. These are caused by sunlight being bent through ice crystals in clouds high up.

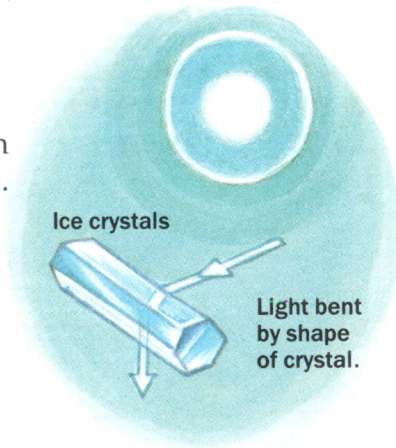

Ice crystals

Light bent by shape of crystal.

Mirages

Mirages are often seen over hot deserts or roads. They are optical illusions, caused by light being bent as it passes from a layer of cold air into a layer of warm air. The warm layer makes the light bend and you see a mirror image of the sky, which looks like water.

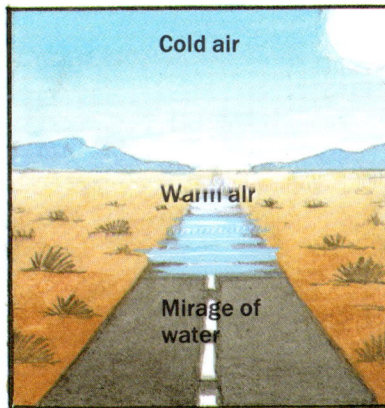

Cold air

Warm air

Mirage of water

Coloured snow

Snow in the Alps is occasionally pink, brown or even red! This is caused by coloured dust from the Sahara Desert being swept high up and carried 2,000km by the wind.

There are tiny bugs living in the snow above 3,000m which can also turn the snow pink.

Owzat!

An umpire at a cricket match in 1975 had his false metal leg struck by lightning. He was unhurt, but his knee melted and the joint stuck together!

Ouch!

Giant hailstones, the size of tennis balls, fell in Alabama USA in April 1988, smashing car windscreens.

Raining fish

Waterspouts are like tornadoes over the sea, and last for about an hour. They are swirling columns of air that suck up seawater and even fish and small crabs. Sometimes a waterspout moves onto land and the animals rain down!

Storm cloud

Anticlockwise swirl

Moves forwards at about 20kph

Several waterspouts were seen in the English channel on 18 August, 1974.

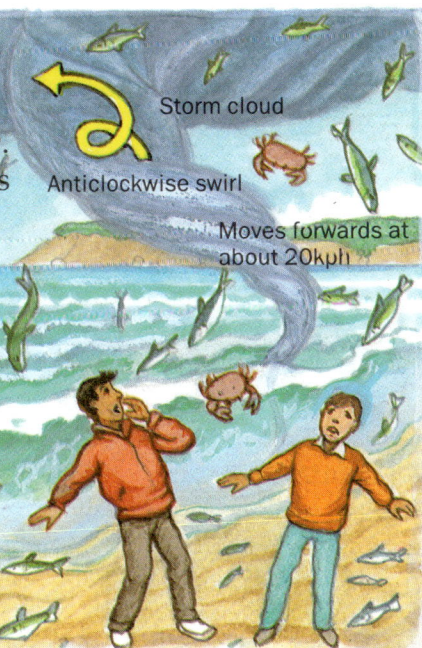

Disaster

Each year there are extremes of weather which bring disasters all round the world. Some cause millions of pounds or dollars worth of damage, but others leave people homeless or even dead.

With planning, some of the effects are sometimes avoided. In the USA, for example, the weather service tries to give up-to-the-minute warnings of approaching tornadoes so that people can take cover.

Too little water

Unexpected drought is a serious problem in many parts of the world. In 1976 the worst drought on record affected California, Britain and Europe. Reservoirs in Britain dried up and water was rationed. Another drought in Mid-West America in 1988 was the worst for 50 years.

Drought in Africa

For the last 20 years there has been an almost constant drought in the Sahel region of Africa. It sometimes rains between July and September, but the rain is quickly washed away, taking the soil with it. The people are unable to grow their crops or feed their animals, and thousands have died of starvation.

Dry, cracked soil in America 1988.

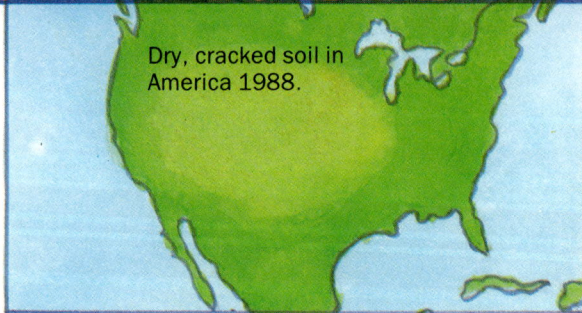

Desert

Sahel region

Wet

Some rain

Desert

Band Aid and other organizations have helped to raise money for the people of the Sahel region to build new life-saving wells and other projects.

Too much water

Floods are very common all round the world. Some cause terrible destruction. A flood caused by a cyclone in Bangladesh in 1970 killed about one million people. Other floods ruin crops and damage property. The 1976 drought in Europe was followed by floods which destroyed the Soviet grain harvest. Sudan and Bangladesh had very severe floods in 1988.

Flood in Sudan

Monsoon

In July each year in Asia there is a monsoon. This is a deluge of rain, caused by winds called the South West Monsoon. They blow over the Indian Ocean and bring rain, which is followed by a dry season. Asian farmers are geared to the monsoon and a delay of just a few weeks can cause droughts and famine.

Worst disasters this century

1900	USA: storm tide kills 6,000 people along the coast of Texas	
1906	Hong Kong: typhoon strikes killing 50,000 people	
1911	Yangtze River, China: floods drown 100,000 people	
1925	USA: tornadoes kill 700 people in one day	
1931	Yangtze River, China: floods drown 150,000 people	
1939	Henan, China: floods kill one million people	
1943	Bengal, India: drought leads to famine and kills one and a half million people	
1952	London: smog kills over 2,500 people	
1953	North Sea coastal areas: storm tide kills 2,000	

1955	USA: hurricane kills 200 people	
1962	Peru: avalanche buries more than 3,000 people	
1963	Bangladesh: cyclone and tidal waves kill 20,000 people	
1966	Florence, Italy: River Arno floods, destroying priceless works of art	
1970	Bangladesh: cyclone and floods kill one million people	
1975	Northeastern Africa: drought leads to famine and kills 50,000 people	
1975	Umtali, Zimbabwe: lightning kills 21 people	
1980+	Sahel region, Africa: drought leads to famine, killing thousands of people	
1988	Sudan: torrential rain causes severe floods, thousands made homeless	

And now the weather...

Every day, all round the world, hundreds of weather forecasts are given out on TV and radio, in newspapers and on telephone and computer networks. All this information comes from meteorological offices – in Britain the London Weather Centre and the main Met Office at Bracknell in Berkshire.

Weather readings from satellites, ships, planes, balloons and weather stations arrive at the meteorological office. You can find out more about this over the page.

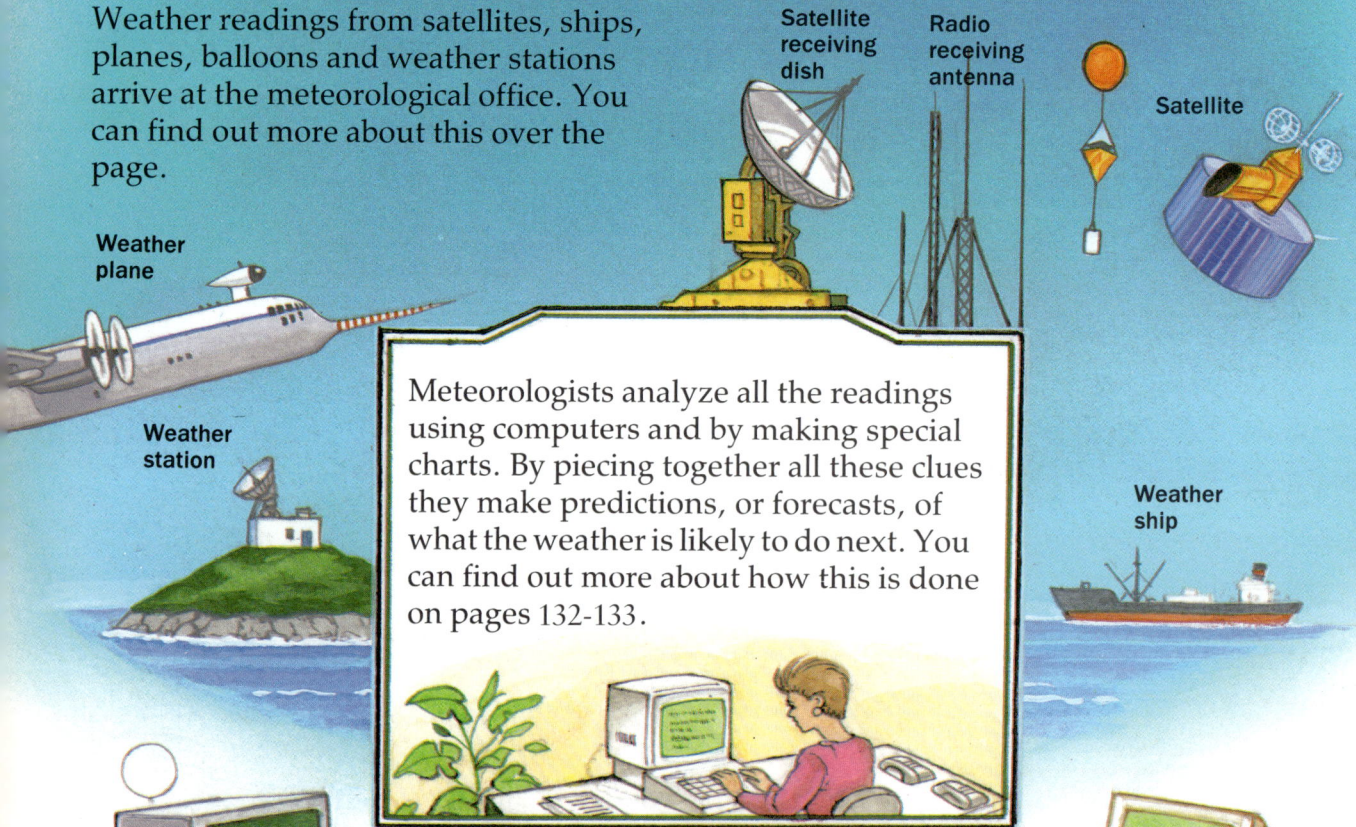

Satellite receiving dish

Radio receiving antenna

Satellite

Weather plane

Weather station

Meteorologists analyze all the readings using computers and by making special charts. By piecing together all these clues they make predictions, or forecasts, of what the weather is likely to do next. You can find out more about how this is done on pages 132-133.

Weather ship

The meteorologists' forecasts are distributed to the different media shown below by telephone, radio, fax or computer links. Some meteorological offices have their own radio or TV studios to broadcast directly to the public. Some BBC Radio weather forecasts, for example, come from a studio at the London Weather Centre.

Television

TV stations broadcast local and national weather forecasts, often using the latest computer graphics techniques.

Computer

Computer information networks, like the BBC's Ceefax service, have up-to-the-minute national forecasts.

Radio

Radio forecasts are especially useful for the merchant navy, who listen out for storm warnings at sea.

Newspapers

Newspapers often show the weather at holiday resorts around the world, as well as giving local forecasts.

Telephone

Telephone companies often give forecasts for very localized areas – useful if you are travelling.

TV maps and symbols

Most television weather maps are created on special-effects computers. The computer can show, or simulate, how clouds are expected to spread the next day, for example. The map shown below is used on BBC1.

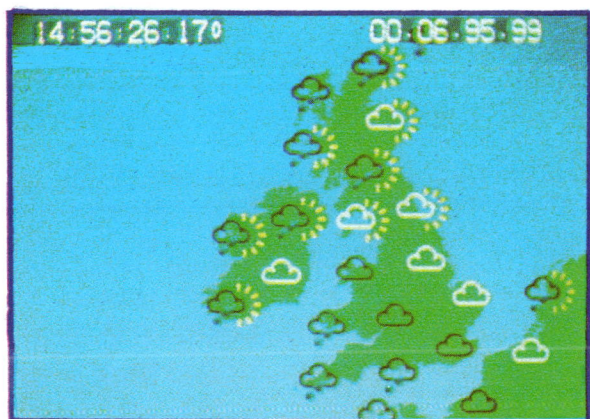

Worldwide weather

The pictures below show how weather maps are shown in different papers around the world.

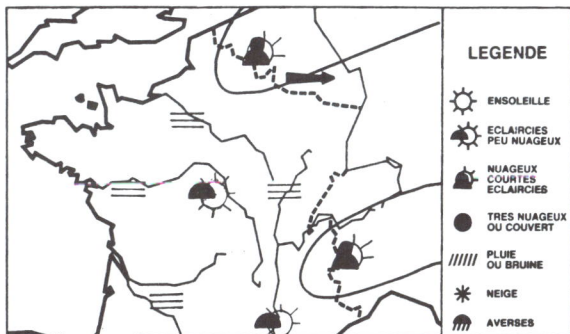

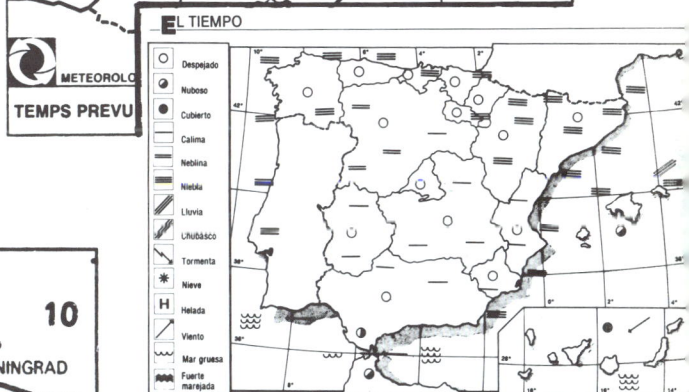

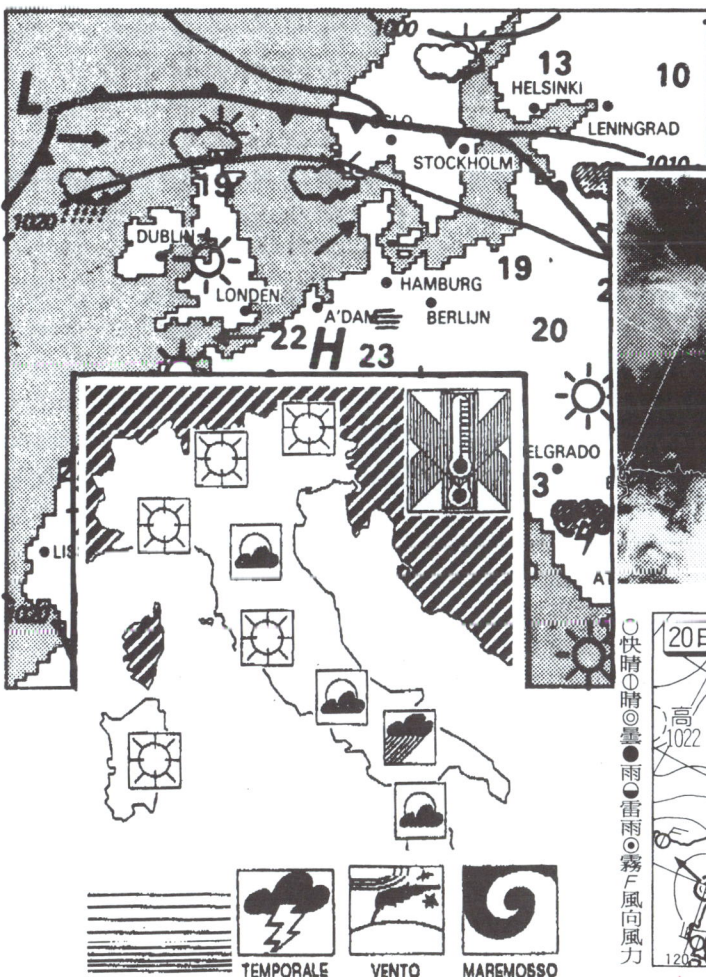

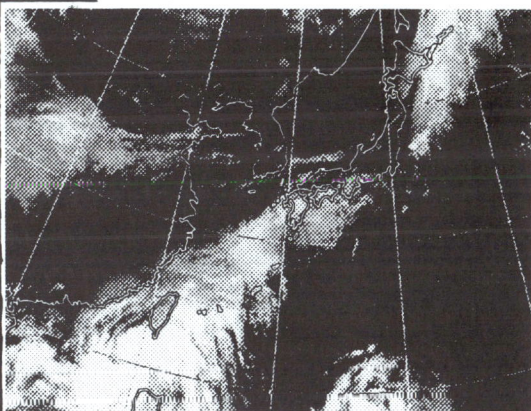

LEGENDE
ENSOLEILLE
ECLAIRCIES PEU NUAGEUX
NUAGEUX COURTES ECLAIRCIES
TRES NUAGEUX OU COUVERT
PLUIE OU BRUINE
NEIGE
AVERSES

METEOROLO
TEMPS PREVU

EL TIEMPO

Despejado
Nuboso
Cubierto
Calima
Neblina
Niebla
Lluvia
Chubasco
Tormenta
Nieve
Helada
Viento
Mar gruesa
Fuerte marejada

TEMPORALE VENTO MAREMOSSO

Weather watch

Weather forecasters are a bit like detectives. They are constantly piecing together clues about the state of the weather now, to work out what might happen next. The word "forecast" was first used by Britain's Chief Meteorologist, Admiral Fitzroy, in 1850. Forecasters have to keep a close watch on the weather. They make their observations using a variety of different equipment.

Gathering information

There are about 10,000 weather stations all over the world. They are linked together in a system called the World Meteorological Organization. Small stations are linked to a "trunk" of main weather centres, shown on this map.

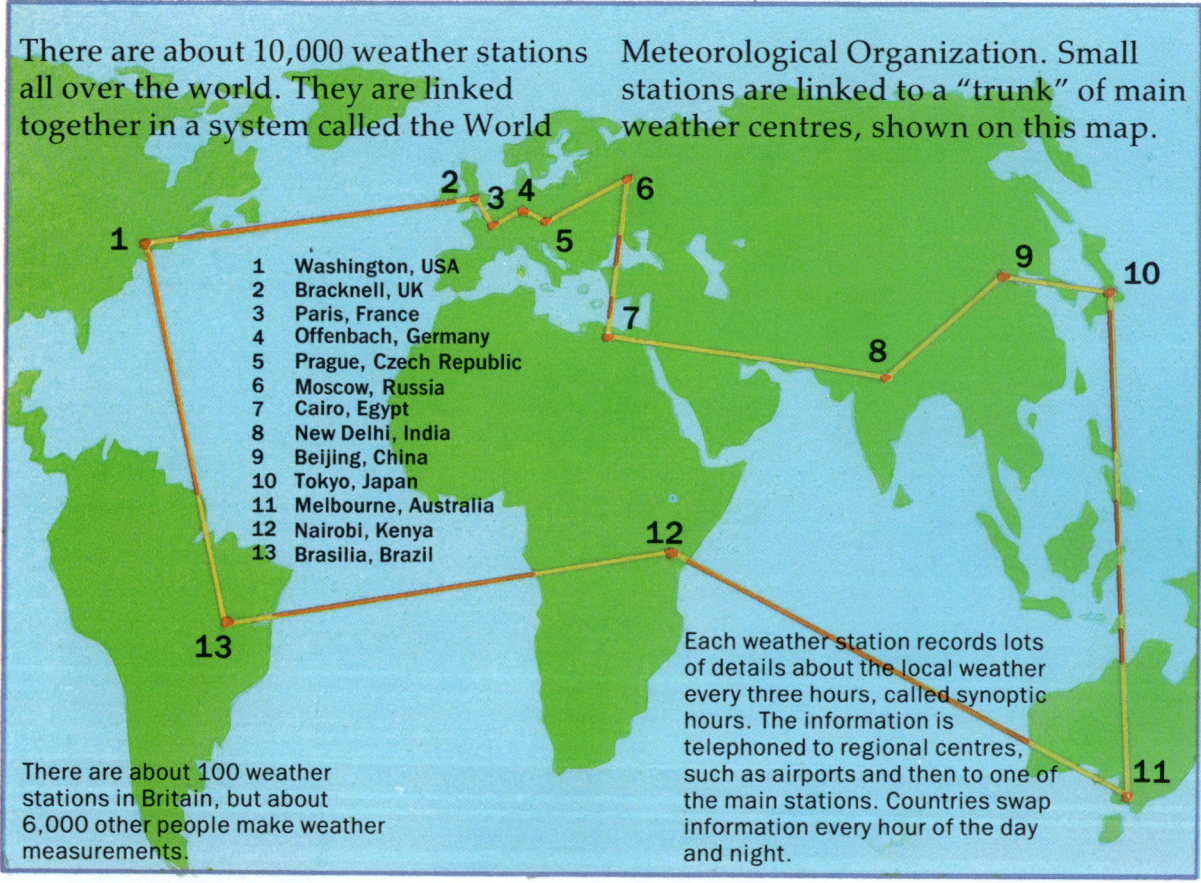

1   Washington, USA
2   Bracknell, UK
3   Paris, France
4   Offenbach, Germany
5   Prague, Czech Republic
6   Moscow, Russia
7   Cairo, Egypt
8   New Delhi, India
9   Beijing, China
10 Tokyo, Japan
11 Melbourne, Australia
12 Nairobi, Kenya
13 Brasilia, Brazil

There are about 100 weather stations in Britain, but about 6,000 other people make weather measurements.

Each weather station records lots of details about the local weather every three hours, called synoptic hours. The information is telephoned to regional centres, such as airports and then to one of the main stations. Countries swap information every hour of the day and night.

What is recorded?

Outside each weather station is a box called a Stevenson screen. This shields the weather recording instruments it contains from direct sunlight.

The meteorologist records details of:

Temperature

Wind direction

Air pressure

Wind strength

Clouds

Humidity

Visibility

Sunshine

Precipitation (rain or snow)

Collecting information

Information about the weather is also gathered in other ways too. The pictures below show some of the main methods used.

Balloons

Balloons are sent about 20km up in the air every day. They carry radio transmitters and send details of temperature and humidity.

These are also called "radiosonde" balloons.

Eventually the balloon bursts and its instruments crash to the ground.

Radar

A network of radars track the progress of rain across the country. Each radar has a range of 200km. Colour-coded patches on the screen show the amount of rain falling.

A radar picture of showers over Britain.

Radars are also used to track the position of tornadoes.

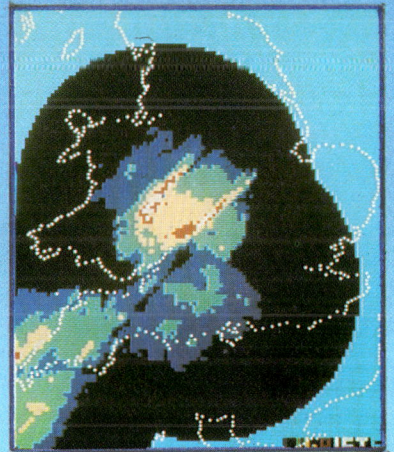

Satellites

Satellites collect information about the atmosphere which cannot be seen from the ground, such as temperature at various heights and cloud coverage over a wide area.

Special aircraft

There are special aircraft fitted with instruments to detect weather conditions. In the USA planes even fly through hurricanes to find out more about them. The UK Meteorological Research plane is called "Snoopy" because its instruments are in a funny nose.

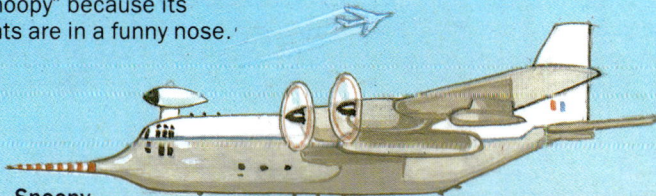

Snoopy

Automatic weather stations

These are often on remote islands, but some are in the countryside. They make automatic measurements and send them by radio or phone lines to main stations.

Automatic weather stations are also on buoys at sea and on some aircraft.

Ships and aircraft

Volunteer crews send reports to weather stations of weather conditions they observe at sea or in the air.

Forecasting

Weather forecasters piece together the information they gather from around the world, then make two sorts of forecasts – short and long range. A special map is drawn, called a synoptic chart, to predict the short range weather 24 hours ahead.

Computers are used to make quite accurate long range forecasts as much as 8 days ahead. Scientists think that by the year 2020 it will be possible to make accurate forecasts up to 14 days ahead.

Who needs a forecast?

You might want to know what the weather will be like tomorrow if you want to go to the beach, for example. But companies need accurate forecasts to help them plan their work. Each day, a country's meteorological service sells special weather information to organizations such as those shown below.

Airlines

Airlines save money on fuel by getting their pilots to avoid strong headwinds, which slow down the plane, and by flying at the best height for the weather.

Farmers

Farmers need to know the best time to sow, spray, water or harvest their crops. Pesticides, for example, are wasted if the farmer uses them just before it rains.

Construction companies

Frost spoils new concrete, rain makes earth-moving difficult and big cranes are dangerous to use in strong winds. Builders check the weather to plan what they should do.

Supermarkets

Supermarkets will buy lots of extra salad vegetables, cold drinks and ice cream if hot weather is forecast. People buy more of these things in a hot spell.

Making a forecast

The forecaster uses the latest information on pressure, wind, temperature, rainfall, cloud cover and so on to draw the synoptic chart. This gives the best clues about what might happen next. The synoptic chart uses isobars – points of equal pressure linked together in lines – to tell you about lows, highs and fronts.

Fronts

Fronts are boundaries between different masses of air. There are four main kinds of airmass, shown on the map below, which are named after the kind of climate they come from. The weather is often very unsettled near fronts, with rain and clouds. There are three sorts of fronts: warm, cold and occluded.

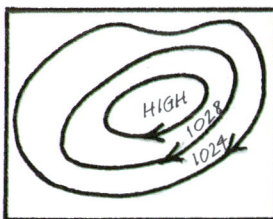

Highs

High-pressure areas, called anticylones, bring dry, settled weather. Any winds blow clockwise in these areas.

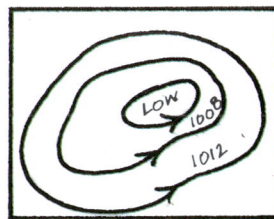

Lows

Low-pressure areas, called depressions, bring cloud and rain. The winds blow anti-clockwise in these areas.

Air masses

Polar continental (cold and dry, especially in winter) – formed over northern Canada and USSR

Polar maritime (cool damp air) – formed over the cold northern seas.

Tropical continental (hot and dry air) – formed over hot areas of Africa, Asia and Mexico.

Tropical maritime (warm damp air) – formed over warm seas near the equator.

Equator

Warm fronts

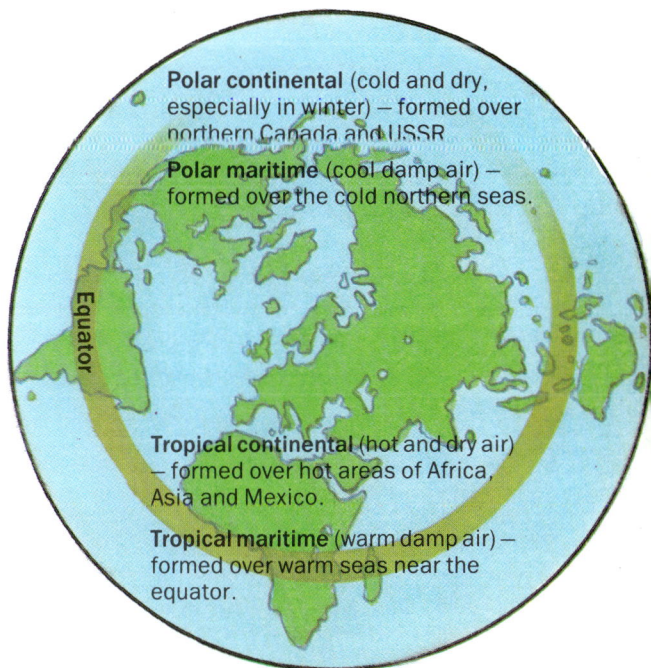

Warm fronts are when warm air advances and rides up over cold air.

From above   **From the side**

These symbols mean warm front

Warm air

Cold air

Rain or snow for about 250km

Cold fronts

A cold front is when cold air pushes under warm air.

From above   **From the side**

These symbols mean cold front.

Cumulonimbus clouds along the front

Cold air

Warm air

Cold air

Showers for 300km, heavy rain for 80km

Occluded fronts

Occluded fronts are when cold air has advanced on warm air and lifted it.

From above   **From the side**

These symbols mean occluded front.

Cold air

Warm air

Cool air

Warm air

Cold air

Cool air

Rain

Weather station

You might like to set up your own weather station and keep a record of the weather. Here is how to make the equipment you need to measure wind direction and speed, temperature and pressure. There is a rain gauge to make on page 114. It is a good idea to take readings at the same time each day, otherwise it will be difficult to compare the results from one day to another.

Wind direction

You can measure wind direction with this simple wind vane. It works just like a weather cock on a church tower.

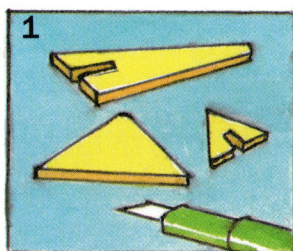

You need:

Some sheets of balsa wood (or thin plywood if you want your wind vane to last longer).

A nail

2 plastic beads (nail must fit holes loosely)

Balsa glue

Hammer

Craft knife

A compass

1 Cut the pieces for the wind vane as shown above.

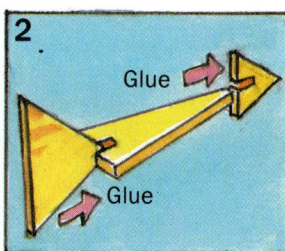

2 Glue the pieces together as shown.

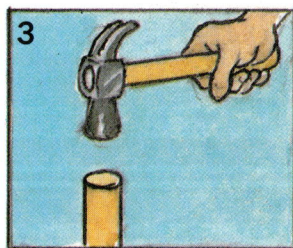

Glue

Glue

Remember that wind direction is the direction the wind is blowing from.

3 Find a wooden fence post, or bang one into the ground.

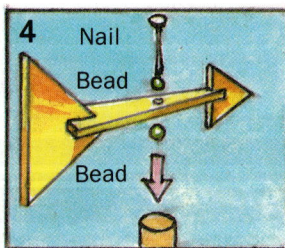

4 Fix the wind vane to the post as shown.

Nail
Bead
Bead

5 Mark north where south should be, east where west should be, and so on.

6 The arrow will point towards the direction the wind is blowing from.

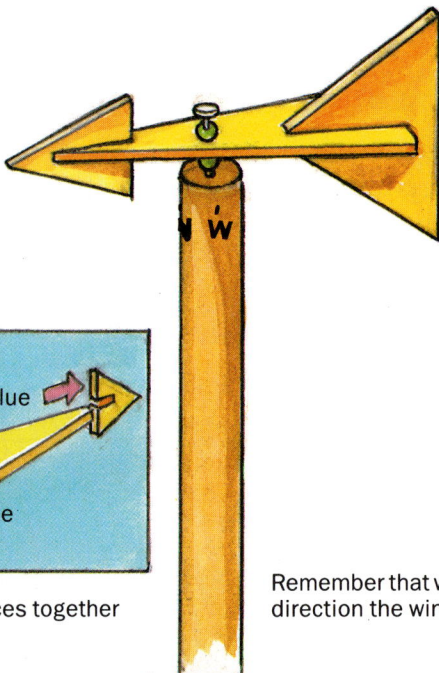

Temperature

Air flows through the open ends.

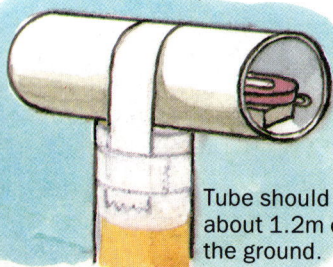

Tube should be about 1.2m off the ground.

To take the temperature you need an ordinary household thermometer, but it must be kept in a shaded place outside. Meteorologists use a special shade called a Stevenson screen (see page 130). You can make a simple shade to protect your thermometer from direct sunlight.

You need:

Thermometer

Plastic bottle

1.5m wooden post

2 matchboxes

White emulsion paint and brush

Scissors

Hammer   Sticky tape

1 Cut the ends off the bottle to make a tube.

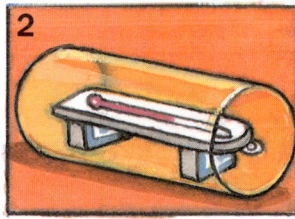

2 Place the thermometer inside the tube, balanced on matchboxes.

3 Bang the post into the ground and tape the tube to it. Remove the thermometer to take a reading.

4 Paint the tube white. This will reflect direct sunlight.

Air pressure

Meteorologists use a barometer to measure air pressure (see page 109). This simple barometer will detect whether the pressure is rising or falling.

You need:
A clear tall plastic bottle
Brick
Ink or powder paint
Water
Sticky tape
Sticky label
Shallow plastic dish
Someone to help

1 Colour some cold water with ink or powder paint and three-quarters fill the bottle.

2 Put your finger over the bottle and turn it upside down into the dish. Keep the bottle upright.

3 Tape the bottle to the brick as shown and mark the water level with the sticky label.

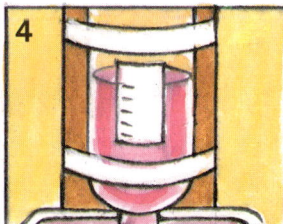

4 The water level rises as the air pressure rises, and falls as the pressure falls.

Wind speed

Wind speed is measured with an instrument called an anemometer. You can make a simple one of your own quite easily.

You need:
About 30cm of strong thread or fishing line
Sticky tape
Ping-pong ball
Protractor – the bigger the better
Someone to help

1 Tape one end of the thread to the protractor and the other to the ping-pong ball.

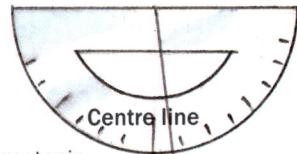

2 Hold the anemometer in the wind outside and ask a friend to read the angle on the protracter.

3 This chart shows roughly how strong the wind is in kilometres per hour:

Angle	90°	80°	70°	60°	50°	40°	30°	20°
Speed in kph	0	13	19	24	29	34	41	52

Weather notebook

You could record the weather each day in a notebook drawn out like the one below. Take notes on wind direction and speed, temperature, pressure, rainfall, sunshine and cloud cover.

Weather long ago

About 20,000 years ago, most of northern Britain was covered in a thick sheet of ice hundreds of metres thick – the last ice age. Since then, the climate has become warmer and the ice has melted to cover just the north and south poles. Scientists think that we are now in a warm part of another ice age, which could last 50,000 years or so.

Water levels

As the Earth's climate slowly changes over many centuries, the ice at the poles gets thicker or thinner. The sea has risen about 100m over the last 10,000 years as the ice has melted. There is enough ice left at the poles to make the sea rise another 100m. This would be deep enough to flood London, New York, Sydney and many other low-lying towns and cities.

The last 7,000 years

5,000-2,000 BC

The weather was much warmer than it is now. This lasted until Roman times. The weather was warm enough in Britain, for example, for the occupying Romans to be able to grow grapes.

1600-1800 AD

A cold period occurred called the "little ice age". Glaciers, sheets of ice on mountains, got thicker, and rivers in Europe froze over every winter. The ice on the Thames was so thick, that "frost fairs" were held.

1800-1900 AD

The temperature began to rise again. The bodies of climbers who had fallen to their deaths in Victorian times were found as mountain glaciers melted a little.

1900-today

Scientists think that temperatures have dropped about 0.5°C. Pollution is now threatening the natural changes. Oddly, 1987 was the warmest year worldwide this century.

Why does the climate change?

Natural changes in the world's climate are always gradually taking place. There are many reasons for this, but scientists think that things such as volcanic eruptions and wobbles in the Earth's tilt are mainly to blame.

Wobbles

The Earth orbits the Sun at an angle called its axis. Sometimes the planet wobbles on its axis and this affects the amount of sunlight reaching the surface.

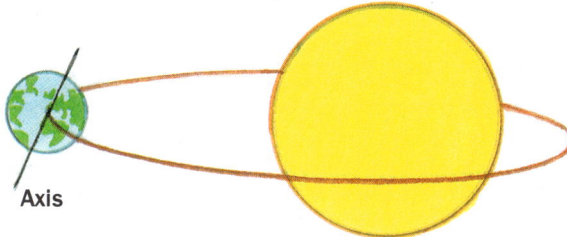

Axis

This shape of this orbit is called an ellipse.

Volcanoes

Millions of tonnes of dust are thrown into the atmosphere when a large volcano erupts. In 1883 the Krakatoa volcano exploded and the dust stayed in the air for three years. This affected the climate because less sun could shine through the darkened skies.

Krakatoa, between Java and Sumatra.

Testing change

Scientists have different ways of finding out what the climate used to be like.

Fossils

Fossils sometimes contain things such as seeds which give clues about the kind of climate at the time the fossil was formed.

Tree rings

Each ring on a tree is a record of the kind of weather at the time the ring was formed. Thick rings show that the weather was warm that year, for example.

Fossilized remains of tree stumps showing their annual growth rings have been found.

Historical records

The ancient Romans, Chinese and Greeks kept weather records and also noted when crops were harvested. Detailed records have been kept for Europe and the USA since about 1700 AD.

End of the dinosaurs

Some scientists think that the dinosaurs died out about 65 million years ago because of changes in the climate. One idea is that a meteor struck the Earth, causing a giant dust cloud which blocked the Sun's heat. Dinosaurs are thought to have been cold blooded, so they would have frozen to death.

What is happening to the weather?

Many adults remember the weather being different in their childhood, compared to how it is now, with snow at Christmas and long, hot summers. Is this just memories of happy times, or is the weather really changing? Most scientists think that it is, although they don't all agree what kind of changes will happen or what the causes are. Many people believe that pollution is to blame, but there are different theories about the effects of the world's car fumes, power station smoke and industrial waste.

Holes in the sky

In 1985, scientists at the British Antarctic Survey discovered that there were thin patches, or "holes", in the ozone layer of the atmosphere over Antarctica. Ozone is a protective gas cloud 10-60km up in the atmosphere. It keeps out harmful rays from the sun and prevents the Earth from getting too hot. The holes are thought to be caused by too many waste gases called chlorofluorocarbons – CFCs for short – escaping from aerosols, plastic foam cartons and many other industrial products.

CFCs escape from burger cartons when they are crushed.

What does it mean for the weather?

The earth seems to be getting hotter – perhaps as a result of extra heat from the sun getting through the damaged ozone layer. This could mean that the polar ice caps will melt, and that rainfall and wind patterns will change. Latest forecasts are that average world temperatures could increase by as much as 5°C over the next 100 years.

Greenhouse effect

Since the industrial revolution in the 18th century, there has been a 25% increase in the amount of carbon dioxide in the atmosphere. Carbon dioxide is a gas. The extra amount has come from things such as factory smoke, car exhausts and the burning down of the world's rain forests.

The carbon dioxide forms a cloud around the earth which allows the sun's rays through, but prevents the heat from escaping back into space. This acts like the glass in a greenhouse by trapping the warm air inside, making the earth hotter and hotter.

What does it mean for the weather?

The polar ice caps are likely to melt over many years, but meanwhile the weather could be very unpredictable. Changes in rainfall patterns over the next 100 years could make northern Europe wetter and southern Europe and Africa even drier than it is now.

El Nino

El Nino is a current of water in the southern Pacific ocean. It is usually very cold, but every few years it warms up – nobody knows why. Some scientists think that when this happens, the weather behaves very oddly in the Far East and western USA. These scientists argue that El Nino is more important than the greenhouse effect or holes in the ozone layer.

What does it mean for the weather?

There is not much to prove that El Nino has any effect in Europe, but some people think that Asian and American weather becomes more extreme when El Nino heats up.

Acid rain

Waste gases, such as sulphur dioxide and nitrogen oxides, and small particles from power stations and car exhausts, are dissolved in rainwater. This turns the rain into an acid – often as strong as lemon juice. Pollution from one country is often blown by the wind to make acid rain in a neighbouring country.

What does it mean for the weather?

Acid rain does not affect the weather directly, but it does kill trees, poison lakes and damage crops. Trees absorb the gas carbon dioxide, so less trees means more carbon dioxide in the atmosphere, adding to the greenhouse effect. Acid rain also destroys buildings because it eats into the stonework.

A forest devastated by acid rain.

Weather records

Most snow
Silver Lake, Colorado, USA
930mm in 24 hours, April 1921

Least sunshine
North pole
None at all for about 186 days
each winter

Longest lasting rainbow
North Wales
Over 3 hours, August 1979

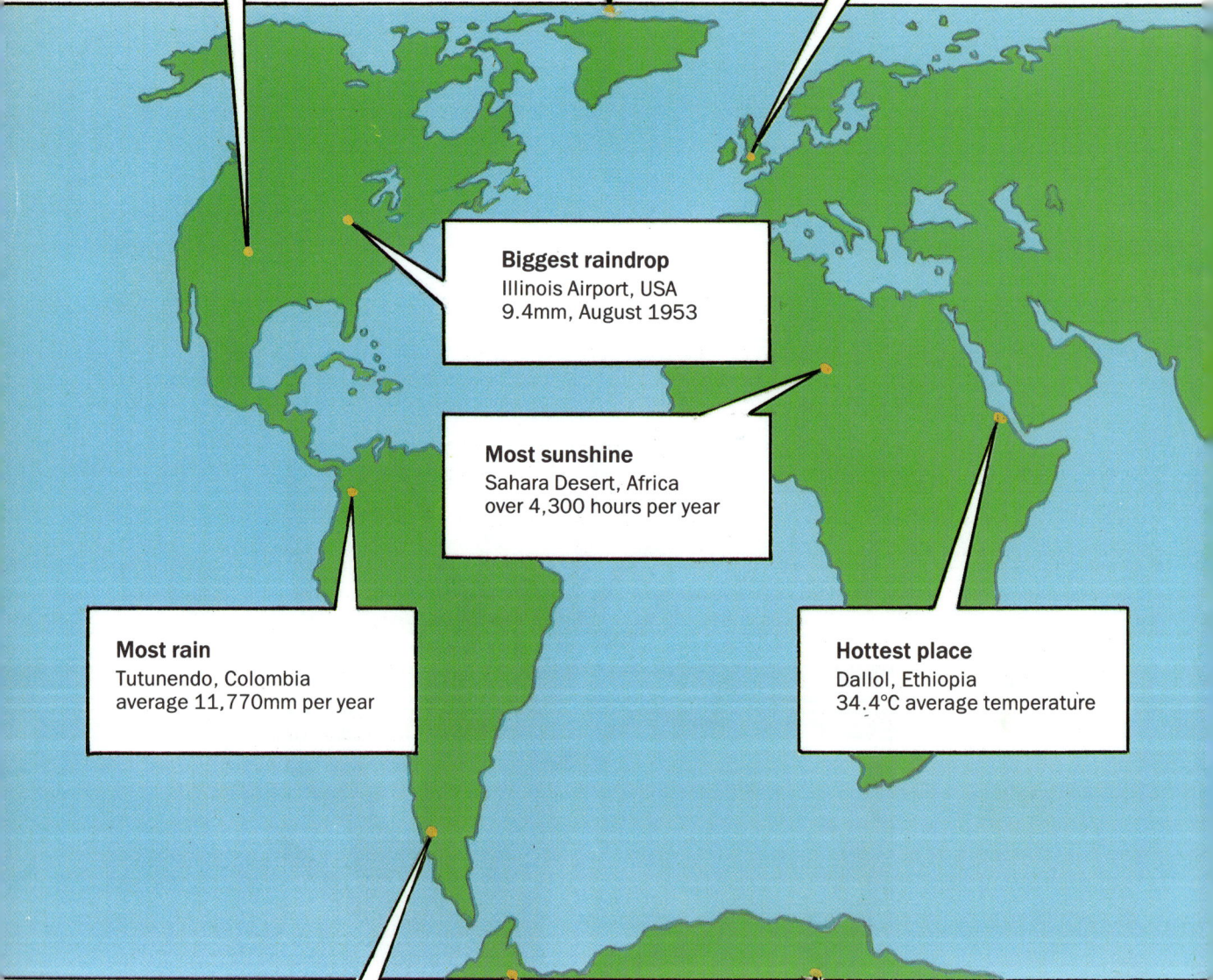

Biggest raindrop
Illinois Airport, USA
9.4mm, August 1953

Most sunshine
Sahara Desert, Africa
over 4,300 hours per year

Most rain
Tutunendo, Colombia
average 11,770mm per year

Hottest place
Dallol, Ethiopia
34.4°C average temperature

Longest drought
Atacama Desert, Chile
about 400 years

Coldest place
Vostock, Antarctica
-89.2°C, July 1983

Windiest place
George V Coast, Antarctica
320kph gales

Acid rain: Rain which is a very weak acid. It is too weak to harm people, but may damage trees and buildings.

Air mass: A region of warm or cold, moist or dry air.

Air pressure: The weight of the Earth's atmosphere pressing down on the surface.

Anemometer: An instrument for measuring wind speed and direction.

Anticyclone: Another name for a high pressure area.

Atmosphere: The gases surrounding the Earth.

Barometer: An instrument for measuring atmospheric pressure.

Beaufort scale: A scale of wind speeds.

Climate: The weather over a period of time in one place.

Cold front: The boundary between two airmasses where the cold air is advancing. Usually brings a spell of rain followed by cooler but brighter weather.

Condensation: When water vapour cools and turns into water.

Cyclone: Another name for a low pressure area, but normally used only in tropical areas.

Depression: Another name for a low pressure area.

Dew point: The temperature at which the water vapour in the air condenses to form droplets.

Greenhouse effect: The warming of the Earth caused by a cloud of pollution preventing the Sun's heat from escaping to space.

Hail: A particle of ice which sometimes are formed in cumulonimbus clouds.

Humidity: The amount of moisture in the air

Hurricane: A very powerful swirling storm.

Isobars: Lines drawn on a map linking points of equal pressure.

Lightning: An electrical charge which jumps from cloud to cloud or from a cloud to the ground.

Occluded front: A band of cloud and rain – like a mixture of a cold and a warm front.

Rain: Liquid water drops falling from the sky. Called drizzle if the drops are tiny.

Shower: Rain falling from a cumulonimbus cloud. Usually lasts less than an hour.

Snow: Ice crystals falling from the sky. Called hail if the crystals are joined as hard lumps.

Thermometer: An instrument for measuring temperature (how hot or cold it is).

Thunderstorm: A storm with thunder and lightning.

Stevenson screen: A white box which protects weather instruments from the direct heat of the Sun.

Warm front: Boundary between two airmasses where the warm air is advancing. Usually brings a spell of rain followed by warmer, moist air.

Water vapour: Water in the form of a gas.

Wind vane: A simple instrument for measuring wind direction.

Published by BBC Educational Publishing, a division of BBC Enterprises Limited, Woodlands, 80 Wood Lane, London W12 0TT

First published in this form 1997
© Tony Potter 1989
Devised and produced by Tony Potter for BBC Enterprises Ltd

Typeset by TDR, Dartford, England
Origination by Dot Gradations, Essex
Printed for Imago in Singapore
ISBN 0 563 37622 8

Acknowledgements
Consultant Editor: Dick File
Designed by Teresa Foster

Illustrations: © Robin Lawrie 1989

Photos: B. Angrove/Barnaby's Picture Library **p. 98;** Australian Information Service/Frank Lane Picture Agency **p. 122;** BBC/L'Unita/El Pais/Le Monde /De Telegraaf **p. 129 (top);** T.A.M. Bradbury **p. 119 (top);** Colin Crane **p. 123 (right);** Earth Satellite Corporation/Science Photo Library **p.96;** Dick File **pp. 113 (top left, centre right), 132 (bottom left and right);** Chris Gilbert **pp. 104 (bottom left), 119 (bottom), 123 (bottom left);** G. Holman **p. 132 (centre right);** Tony Potter **pp. 112, 132 (centre left, bottom left and right);** C. J. Richards **p. 116;** Chris Rose/ICCE **p. 139;** Topsham Picture Library **pp. 102 (top and bottom), 104 (bottom right), p.107 (bottom left and right), 125, 126 (left, right and bottom);** F. Alan Wood **p. 106**

Cover photos: Science photo library/NASA (main picture); Telegraph Colour Library/Planet Earth/Doug Perrine (inset picture)